D0290597

Adolf Hitler

and

Nazi Germany

ADOLF HITLER

AND
NAZI
GERMANY

Earle Rice Jr.

MORGAN
REYNOLDS
PUBLISHING
Greensboro, North Carolina

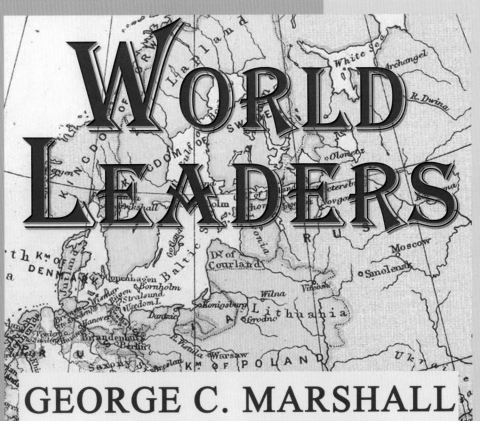

WORLD LEADERS

GEORGE C. MARSHALL
ADOLF HITLER
WOODROW WILSON
VACLAV HAVEL
GENGHIS KHAN
JOSEPH STALIN
CHE GUEVARA

ADOLF HITLER AND NAZI GERMANY

Copyright © 2006 by Earle Rice Jr.

Library of Congress Cataloging-in-Publication Data

Rice, Earle.
Adolf Hitler and Nazi Germany / Earle Rice, Jr.— 1st ed.
p. cm.
Includes bibliographical references and index.
Audience: Ages 10+
ISBN-10: 1-931798-78-8 (library binding)
ISBN-13: 978-1-931798-78-5 (library binding)
1. Hitler, Adolf, 1889-1945—Juvenile literature. 2. Heads of
state—Germany—Biography—Juvenile literature. 3.
Germany—History—1933-1945—Juvenile literature. 4. National
socialism—History—Juvenile literature. I. Title.
DD247.H5R52 2005
943.086'092—dc22

2005017825

Printed in the United States of America
First Edition

⚔ Contents

Adolf Hitler.
(Courtesy of the Granger Collection.)

One

EARLY LIFE

Adolf Hitler was the fourth child born to Alois and Klara Hitler, on April 20, 1889, an Easter Saturday evening. Each of the first three children—Gustav, born in 1885; Ida, born in 1886; Otto, born in 1887— had died before reaching the age of two. The new child's name was entered as Adolfus on his birth certificate, but he was referred to as Adolf. After Adolf, Klara had two more children: Edmund, in 1894, and Paula, in 1896. Alois Hitler had two illegitimate children—Alois Jr. and Angela— rounding out the Hitler family.

The death of her first three children had traumatized Klara Hitler. She doted on young Adolf, whom she considered to be a sickly child, and lived in constant fear of his dying. A kindly woman with long, neatly plaited

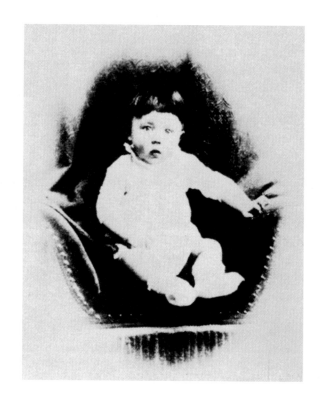

*Christened Adolfus Hitler,
Adolf was the first of his
parents' children to live
beyond the age of two.*
(National Archives)

brown hair and expressive blue-gray eyes set in a long, oval face, Klara devoted herself to her children and stepchildren, all of whom adored her. Adolf's love for her was "his most striking feature," according to Eduard Bloch, Klara's doctor: "While he was not a 'mother's boy' in the usual sense, I have never witnessed a closer attachment."

Young Adolf did not hold his authoritarian father in the same high esteem. Alois worked as a customs inspector, which placed him squarely in the ranks of the lower middle class, and wore a uniform to work each day. Much older than Klara—he had been married and widowed twice before marrying her—Alois Hitler ruled over his family like a tyrant, often lashing out in drunken rages at his children and wife. "It was especially my brother Adolf who challenged my father to extreme harshness and who got his sound thrashing every day," wrote Paula years later. Adolf Hitler learned at a very young age that the one who wields the greatest power prevails.

Before Adolf was three, the Hitler family had moved several times within the village of Braunau, which lay on the border between Austria and Germany. Then, in 1892, Alois received a promotion that reassigned him to Passau, located at the confluence of the rivers Inn and Danube. Adolf loved living in Passau, on the German

Although a tyrannical figure in his son's childhood, Alois Sr.'s avid Austrian patriotism and commitment to public service provided young Adolf with a strong nationalist model that would influence him for the rest of his life. (National Archives)

A devoted if overprotective mother, Klara Hitler had a very close relationship with her son Adolf. (National Archives)

side of the Inn, where he acquired a Bavarian accent that would mark his speech for the rest of his life. Two years later, Alois Sr. received another promotion and a transfer to Linz, back in Austria. Klara was then pregnant with Edmund, so she and the children remained behind in Passau for about a year, much to Adolf's delight. He ran freely around the house without having to worry about his father's reprimands. Sometimes he spent his day playing cowboys and Indians—stories of the American West were popular during this era in Germany and Austria—or war games.

In 1895, at the age of fifty-eight, Alois Sr. retired from the customs service and bought a small farm near the hamlet of Hafeld, a small community with about one hundred inhabitants. The village sat on a high ridge with a fine view of the Salzkammergut Mountains and formed part of the community of Fischlham, near Lambach, some thirty miles southwest of Linz. In his retirement, Alois Sr. began to drink more heavily. There may have been repeated incidents of domestic violence in the Hitler household. Alois Jr. considered Hafeld boring and, after a final beating from his father, ran away from home at the age of fourteen, never to return. Adolf learned to navigate the conflict between his inconsistent father and overindulgent mother to get his way. When he failed to successfully manipulate his parents, he threw a fit.

The area where Alois Sr. chose to retire, near the Salzkammergut Mountains, was a strikingly beautiful yet remote place. (Library of Congress)

Later in life, Hitler would consider the provincial city of Linz to be the ideal model for the German empire, and would often cast it in contrast to Vienna, the city he would come to know and hate as a young adult. (Library of Congress)

Adolf entered the *Volksschule* (public school) in nearby Fischlham at the age of six. He would later recall, "Schoolwork was ridiculously easy, leaving me so much free time that the sun saw more of me than my room." In 1897, the always-discontented Alois Sr. sold his property in Hafeld and moved his family to Lambach. There Adolf attended the Benedictine monastery school and, for a time, aspired to the priesthood.

The Hitlers moved again in 1898, this time to Leonding, a village of about 3,000 people on the outskirts of Linz, where Alois Sr. bought a spacious house with a tile roof and two chimneys on about a half-acre of land. The family now consisted of Klara, Adolf,

Edmund, and Paula. Adolf loved living close to Linz, which had provincial theaters, an opera house, and government buildings. To the end of his days, he would think of it as his hometown.

A class picture taken in Leonding in 1899 shows Adolf in the topmost center of his group with his chin up and arms crossed, suggesting a rebellious air of cocky self-assurance. In addition to breezing through his studies with little effort, he was now experiencing an artistic awakening and began to sketch in class on the sly. On one occasion, a classmate watched in wonder as Adolf, from memory, produced on paper a remarkably detailed and accurate rendering of the castle of Schaumberg. Adolf's aspirations to become an artist

Adolf's class picture from 1899. He stands in the center of the back row.

placed him in yet another conflict with his father.

Adolf was fascinated with the frontier tales of James Fenimore Cooper and the Wild West narratives of his German imitator, Karl May, an ex-convict from Saxony who had never been to America. In more than seventy novels, May created imaginary settings in Texas, Arizona, and New Mexico to serve as backgrounds for his action hero, Old Shatterhand, whose exploits held a generation of German and Austrian boys in thrall. "I owe to Karl May my first ideas of geography," Adolf said later, "and the fact he opened my eyes to the world." The future dictator learned much of his distorted sense of American and Middle Eastern geography—which he carried with him throughout his life—from a writer who never set foot outside of Germany and invented as he wrote. At recess and after school, Adolf tirelessly led his classmates in reenactments of May's scenarios, casting himself in the role of Old Shatterhand, who perpetually fought wars against "inferior" races and sent them to their doom.

Around this time, Adolf further stimulated his interest in warfare by reading a pair of illustrated magazines that documented the Franco-Prussian War of 1870–71. One result of that war between France and Prussia had been the unification of the dozens of independent German states into one nation. "From then on I became more and more enthusiastic about everything that was in any way connected with war or, for that matter, with soldiering," he wrote later.

Soon after the turn of the new century, Adolf's care-free days of play soldiering ended. On February 2, 1900, while Adolf was completing his last year in Volksschule, his brother Edmund died of measles at the age of six. No one knows just how close Adolf was with his younger brother, but Edmund's death struck him and the rest of the family very hard. With Alois Jr. gone, Alois Sr. began to concentrate more of his undesired attention on Adolf. He wanted his remaining son to prepare for a career as a civil servant, to follow in his footsteps. Adolf had already made up his mind to become an artist; the conflict intensified.

On September 17, 1900, Adolf, eleven, entered *Realschule* (secondary school) in Linz. The Realschule emphasized technical and scientific studies, whereas the *Gymnasium* (also a secondary school) stressed a classical curriculum aimed at preparing students for university. Adolf was eligible to attend either school, but his father enrolled him in the more practical Realschule. Adolf did not protest because Realschule offered a course in drawing.

Adolf's performance in secondary school, however, was poor. His urban classmates tended to look down on him as unsophisticated. In a class picture taken that year, he again appeared in the top row, but a sadly forlorn figure now replaced the cocky, self-assured youngster of a year earlier. Adolf withdrew into a shell, showed little interest in his schoolwork, and failed to earn pro-motion his first year. Reflecting on it much later, he

Adolf (back row, far right), *his haughty stature diminished, in a class picture from 1903.* (Library of Congress)

excused himself for his academic shortcomings. "I thought that once my father saw how little progress I was making at the *Realschule*," he later wrote, "he would let me devote myself to my dream, whether he liked it or not."

On the morning of January 3, 1903, Alois Hitler Sr. set out on his morning walk and was stricken with a pleural (lung) hemorrhage. He died moments later in the arms of a neighbor at the Gasthaus Stiefler, a nearby inn and tavern. Despite past differences, when thirteen-year-old Adolf viewed his father's body, he broke down and wept.

Adolf continued to do poorly at the Linz school. In 1904, his grades finally forced him to transfer to the state secondary school at Steyr, about fifty miles away. He hated Steyr and left without graduating in 1905, at the age of sixteen.

For the next few years, Adolf's greatest talent was his ability to avoid work or responsibility. A pension left to Klara and the children by Alois Sr. enabled the family to maintain a comfortable living in a rented flat on the Humboldtstrasse in Linz. Adolf idled away the hours, roaming the streets, attending the theater and the opera, and frequenting the library, where he began to read voraciously in German history and mythology. Much of his eclectic education was self-administered. He had a lifelong contempt for educators, of whom he later wrote, "The majority of them were somewhat mentally deranged, and quite a few ended their days as honest-to-God lunatics."

One teacher at the Linz Realschule, Dr. Leopold Pötsch, Adolf's history professor, was the exception. Dr. Pötsch was an avid—some say fanatical—German nationalist, who fascinated Adolf with stories of German historical glories. Hitler later recalled him as a "grayhaired man who, by the fire of his narratives, sometimes made us forget the present," who "used our budding nationalistic fanaticism as a means of educating us, frequently appealing to our sense of national honor." This strong sense of German nationalism, mixed with his fascination with artistic romanticism, stirred young Adolf's imagination. He was also developing a keen interest in politics, particularly opposition to the Habsburg family that ruled the vast but rickety Austro-Hungarian Empire. "And indeed, though [Pötsch] had no such intention," Hitler recalled, "it was then that I became a little revolutionary."

Adolf's friend during these years was August Kubizek. "Gustl," as he was called, shared Adolf's love for the operas of Richard Wagner. When the two had money they went to the opera in Linz, but most of their time together was spent walking around while Adolf lectured Gustl on opera or German history. Kubizek was a trained pianist and had vague plans of going to Vienna for more training.

Hitler had little of the carefree spirit of youth. Increasingly bitter and introspective, self-centered and fixated on his own dreams but unwilling to put forth the effort necessary to make them come to fruition, he was an unhappy young man. "He saw everywhere only obstacles and hostility," Kubizek later recalled.

In 1906, shortly after his seventeenth birthday, Adolf Hitler went to Vienna. Funded by his mother, he journeyed to the glittering baroque capital of the Austro-Hungarian Empire for a two-month visit. He wandered the streets in a state of constant ecstasy, enthralled by the majestic buildings lining the *Ringstrasse*, the wide, tree-lined boulevard that circled the inner city, and marveling at the museums, theaters, and the opera house.

Everything about the Austrian capital delighted Adolf. Before returning to Linz, he inquired about enrolling at the Vienna Academy of Fine Arts. A year later, in October 1907, he returned to take the entrance examination for the academy's School of Painting. "I was so convinced

Opposite: When Hitler submitted his portfolio to the Vienna Academy of Fine Arts, he included this watercolor of the peaceful Austrian countryside.

that I would be successful that when I received my rejection," he wrote later, "it struck me as a bolt from the blue." The academy examiner told him his portfolio of paintings suggested that his talents lay not in painting but in architecture.

Adolf resolved that he "should some day become an architect." But he could not meet the entrance requirements to the School of Architecture because of his failure to graduate from Realschule. This was another setback, but there was worse to come when he was summoned home by his mother's doctor. Klara Hitler died on December 21, 1907. Dr. Bloch, who was accustomed to deathbed scenes, later recalled, "I have never seen anyone so prostrate with grief as Adolf Hitler."

Adolf later wrote that his mother's death "was a dreadful blow. I had honored my father, but my mother I had loved." He had lost the one person who had provided him with emotional support.

For the first time in his life, Adolf Hitler was on his own. Early in 1908, he left Linz, again headed for Vienna. This time he would not return. As he would later write, he "wanted to become 'something'—but on no account a civil servant." Six years of idle searching lay before him. He would become familiar with the back alleys and homeless hostels of first Vienna and then Munich, in his beloved Germany, before a war put him on the path toward "something."

☙ *Two*

THE AIMLESS YEARS

Hitler arrived in Vienna in February 1908, and would remain there for the next five years. Vienna was one of the cultural centers of Europe. Painters such as Gustav Klimt were creating startlingly new, highly ornate images, while radical composers such as Arnold Schönberg were questioning the tonal underpinnings of western music. Sigmund Freud was seeing patients in his office and beginning to publish articles and books that claimed to penetrate into the deepest unconscious motivations and urges of human beings. Vienna was a magnet for young men eager to embrace change.

There were conflicting social forces in Vienna, however. Culturally, the imperial capital city was embracing the new century; politically, the Austro-Hungarian empire

Hitler came to associate the bustling Austrian city of Vienna with rejection. Embittered and frustrated, he found ways to blame his failure there on the city's diverse population of Jews and foreigners. (Library of Congress)

was ruled by an outdated monarchial government clearly on its last legs. Emperor Franz Joseph had reigned for over sixty years. Now nearly senile, he depended on the advice of corrupt ministers to rule over a crumbling empire composed of a hodgepodge of different ethnic groups. The Poles, Galicians, Ruthenians, Slovaks, Bohemians, Moravians, and Hungarians all longed for their own nations and the right to control their own affairs.

Economically, all of Europe was undergoing rapid, sometimes brutal, change. The new industrial economy had created great wealth, a growing middle class, and brought thousands of people to work in the new factories. These huge, impersonal operations strove for maximum efficiency, which often meant sudden layoffs and low wages. The inept government had no means to help level out the boom and bust cycles, which kept the majority of the population in a state of anxiety.

Hitler came to Vienna, a city he had fallen in love with during his earlier visits, expecting to accomplish great things. When he failed to realize his dreams, he began to blame the city for his failings. Years later, he would write, "To me Vienna . . . represents, I am sorry to say, merely the living memory of the saddest period in my life."

It was during his years in Vienna, from 1908 to 1913, that Hitler crystallized his thinking, and his fanaticism, around the two fixations that would drive him the rest of his life and would eventually push the world into the most destructive war in history. "In this period my eyes were opened to two menaces of which I had previously scarcely known the names," he wrote, "and whose terrible importance for the existence of the German people I certainly did not understand: Marxism and Jewry."

Hitler arrived in the imperial city with a small income from an orphan's pension, plus his share of his mother's modest savings in reserve. He moved into a second-floor room at Stumpergasse 31, near the *Westbahnhof* (railway station), which he rented from a Czech woman named Maria Zakreys. Hitler persuaded Gustl Kubizek to follow him to Vienna to pursue a musical career at the

Hitler's friend from Linz and roommate in Vienna, Gustl Kubizek.

Vienna Conservatoire. Kubizek joined him on February 22, and they moved into a bigger room at the same address. Beyond the simple necessities—two beds, a commode, a wardrobe, a washstand, a table and two chairs—the larger room left enough room for Gustl's rented piano.

Kubizek entered the conservatory, and Hitler continued to drift. Much as he had done in Linz, he spent hours wandering the parks and streets, admiring the architecture, occasionally drawing and painting or, when he had the money, attending theaters and the opera. Sometimes he spent the day in the Hof Library, reading unsystematically about ancient Rome, Eastern religions, yoga, occultism, hypnotism, astrology, Protestantism—whatever caught his fancy at the moment. "In this period," Hitler noted years later, "there took shape within me a world picture and a philosophy which became the granite foundation of all my acts." Apart from his comradeship with Kubizek, Hitler led a solitary life.

In July 1908, Kubizek returned to Linz for the summer. When he returned to Vienna, Hitler had vanished. Hitler had reapplied for admission to the School of Painting at the Vienna Academy of Fine Arts, but this time academy officials refused even to let him take the entrance examination. This rejection apparently rendered Hitler unable to face his friend. He severed relations with Kubizek, as well as with his own relatives, and disappeared into the seedy, bug-ridden rooms and *dosshouses* (flophouses) of Vienna for the next five years.

Beginning in 1909, Hitler lived in the streets and parks during the warm months. The autumn cold forced him to take a bed in a dosshouse called the Asylum for the Shelterless. There he met Reinhold Hanisch, an itinerant laborer from German Bohemia, who later described Hitler at the time of their meeting: "On the very first day there sat next to the bed that had been allotted to me a man who had nothing on except an old torn pair of trousers—Hitler. His clothes were being cleaned of lice, since for days he had been wandering about without a roof and in a terribly neglected condition." Hanisch took pity on his new acquaintance and helped him find work beating carpets, carrying bags outside the railway station, shoveling snow, and doing similar menial labor.

In December, Hitler moved into a hostel for single men at Meldemannstrasse 27, where he would stay for his remaining three years in Vienna. Hanisch soon joined him, and they formed a business partnership. Hitler began to paint postcards, pictures, and posters, which Hanisch sold for enough money to sustain their moderate needs. Their partnership broke up in the summer of 1910 when Hitler suspected Hanisch of siphoning off too much of their profits. Hitler continued to make a modest living with his postcard painting for the rest of his time in Vienna and later in Munich.

Years later, a disgruntled Hanisch remembered his former friend as being lazy and moody. "Over and over again," he recalled, "there were days on which he simply refused to work. Then he would hang around the night shelters, living on the bread and soup that he got there, and discussing politics, often getting involved in heated controversies.

"When he got excited, Hitler couldn't restrain himself," Hanisch further recalled. "He screamed and fidgeted with his hands. But when he was quiet it was quite different; he seemed to have a fair amount of self-control and acted in quite a dignified manner." It seems that a passion for politics was gradually supplanting art as the dominant interest in Hitler's life.

At the time, it was popular in many circles to blame the economic distress that accompanied the new economy on Jewish bankers and merchants. This represented a new variation of the suspicion and intolerance of Jews that had been a part of European culture for centuries. Hitler became intrigued by *völkisch* groups, highly nationalistic societies interested in nature, romanticism, and folklore. Some of the more extreme groups were also anti-Semitic, arguing that Jewish people could not be true Germans. Hitler spent long hours reading about the movement in newspapers and activist materials, and he was quick to enthuse about it to anyone who would listen. Hitler's rants began to earn him a reputation for eccentricity among the other patrons of the hostel.

As his interest in radical politics developed, three political parties attracted most of Hitler's interest—the Austrian Social Democrats, Georg Ritter von Schönerer's Pan-German Nationalists, and Karl Lueger's Christian Social Party.

Hitler quickly came to hate the Social Democrats, who advocated a Socialist form of government that put limits on big business and the granting of autonomy to the larger ethnic groups. He felt they were trying to turn the Austro-Hungarian empire into a Slavic state. Slavs were one of the largest ethnic groups in eastern Europe. Hitler considered them to be a lesser people than the Germans. To give the Slavs too much power would rot the state from within. Further, some of the leaders of the Social Democrats were Jewish, which led Hitler to believe the party's ultimate goal was the destruction of Germany and the creation of a Jewish-controlled world government.

While he detested the ideology of the Social Democrats, Hitler admired their political success and began to study the party's literature, organization, pyschology, and political techniques to better understand how it worked. "The greater insight I gathered into the external character of Social Democracy," he wrote, "the greater became my longing to comprehend the inner core of this doctrine." Hitler concluded that the Social Democrats owed their success to three things: they knew how to organize a mass movement; they were masters at the art of propaganda; and they recognized the value and application of what he termed "spiritual and physical terror."

Hitler considered the Communist ideology of Marxism to be the enemy of Germany and German people. Developed by Karl Marx, Marxism argued that all of society's injustices came from private property and the disparities of wealth that it created. Marx advocated the end of private property. All factories, land, and businesses should be controlled by a government that served each according to his or her need. He rejected nationalism and called for an international revolution led by workers.

In the early twentieth century, Marxism was popular among some workers, intellectuals, union leaders, and others in Europe and the United States. In 1917, Russian Marxists, called Bolsheviks, would overthrow the czar and establish the first Communist dictatorship. There were several Jews prominent in Marxist circles—Marx himself was half Jewish. Soon, Hitler made no distinction between the worldwide Jewish conspiracy he was convinced existed and the international Communist

The work of German philosopher and political economist Karl Marx, including The Communist Manifesto, *provided much of the fodder for what Hitler reacted against when developing his anti-Communist and anti-Semitic ideology.*

movement. It was all one huge threat to Germany's destiny.

The second influence on his developing political ideology was Georg Ritter von Schönerer's Pan-German Nationalist Party, which combined German nationalism with anti-Marxism, anti-Catholicism, and anti-Semitism. Hitler thought Schönerer, a wealthy landlord from the Waldviertel region, was a "profound thinker." He also appreciated Schönerer's support for Pan-Germanism, which argued for the unification of all German-speaking people—no matter where they lived—in one nation. But Hitler saw that Schönerer made a fatal mistake by failing to gain the support of major, established institutions. His attacks on the powerful Catholic Church and the army were mistakes Hitler would avoid in the future. Hitler borrowed Schönerer's use of the medieval greeting *"Heil!"* (Hail!) and his self-designated title of *"führer"*

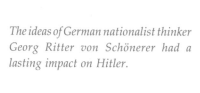

The ideas of German nationalist thinker Georg Ritter von Schönerer had a lasting impact on Hitler.

(leader), which his followers used to address him.

The third political party to attract Hitler's interest was Dr. Karl Lueger's Christian Social Party. Lueger, an anti-Semite, served as Vienna's mayor from 1897 until his death in 1910. Because of his anti-Semitism, Emperor Franz Joseph at first refused to confirm him as mayor but eventually yielded to the will of the people. Hitler later called Lueger the "last great German to be born in the ranks of the people who had colonized the Ostmark [Austria]."

What Hitler most admired about Lueger was his skill at using political tactics and his inclination "to make use of all existing implements of power, to incline mighty existing institutions in his favor, drawing from these old sources of power the greatest possible profit for his own movement." However, he came to distrust Lueger as a political opportunist who used the mass appeal of anti-Semitism more for its political advantage than as a deeply felt belief. Although he was ultimately disappointed by him, Hitler could not deny Lueger's genius in winning mass support, in understanding the problems of modern society, and in recognizing the importance of oratory—Lueger was a dynamic speaker—and propaganda in shaping and swaying public opinion. "If Dr. Karl Lueger had lived in Germany," Hitler noted in *Mein Kampf*, his memoir and political manifesto, "he would have been ranked among the great minds of our people."

It was in Vienna that Hitler became committed to a pathological anti-Semitism. He was even critical of

Vienna mayor Karl Lueger was interested in increasing Christian influence and getting votes, which he did by appealing to lower-class voters through anti-Semitism.

Lueger's "tolerance" of Jews. Although he was no doubt versed in the familiar anti-Semitism easily found in the Austrian countryside of his youth, the available evidence indicates that Hitler did not become a fanatical anti-Semite until he had been in Vienna for some time. He was actually known to have had friendly relations with a few Jews early in his stay while living on Meldemannstrasse. If Hitler's recollections in *Mein Kampf* can be believed, his change of attitude occurred within two years of his exposure to Lueger's politics. He wrote that at some point—he doesn't provide a date— he underwent his "greatest transformation of all." He described it as occurring in a single incident:

> Once, as I was strolling through the Inner City, I suddenly encountered an apparition in a black caftan and black hair locks. Is this a Jew? was my first thought.
>
> For, to be sure, they had not looked like that in Linz. I observed the man furtively and cautiously, but the longer I stared at this foreign face, scrutinizing feature for feature, the more my first question assumed a new form: Is this a German?

After this encounter, Hitler claimed that he began to see Jews in an entirely new light: "Wherever I went, I began to see Jews, and the more I saw, the more sharply they became distinguished in my eyes from the rest of humanity." He developed an interest in anti-Semitic literature and began to project all of his hates and fears onto Jewish people. He eventually convinced himself of the existence of a Jewish-Marxist conspiracy to destroy the German peoples. "If the Jew wins over the world with the help of the Marxists," he wrote, "then this crown will be the wreath of death for mankind."

After his "awakening," Hitler found more and more things to hate—the weak Habsburg regime, the docile working class, the manipulative upper class, the Slavs, all forms of democracy, and anything else he thought was barring the German people from attaining the greatness that was their due. He began to vent his opinions in long-winded harangues in the streets and cheap cafés of Vienna.

By 1913, Hitler had come to despise Vienna, the city that had shattered his dreams and left him destitute. In May, he moved to Munich, in the German state of Bavaria. Hitler later wrote, "Vienna was a hard school for me, but it taught me the most profound lessons of my life."

In the mid-1920s, Hitler would expand upon the lessons and partially formed ideas of his Vienna days and document them in *Mein Kampf*. Later still, the book and its ideas would serve as a blueprint for constructing a new Germany.

In Munich, Hitler continued to obsess over radical politics, still supporting himself by working small jobs and painting. But the new city provided little solace for the lonely, depressed, and embittered man. Hitler's dream of becoming a great artist was gone; he was drifting aimlessly. Some scholars have suggested that he left

The German city of Munich, where Hitler moved to escape Vienna. (Library of Congress)

Vienna to avoid the Austrian draft, but, if true, he failed at that, too. In February 1914, Austrian officials recalled him from Munich and screened him for military service. They found him "too weak and unfit to bear arms."

In August 1914, only five months after Austrian officials had found Hitler unfit for military service, World War I erupted in Europe. Germany was allied with Austria in a war against Russia, Britain, and France. As an Austrian, Hitler had to petition King Ludwig III of Bavaria to request the right to enlist in a Bavarian regiment. When he received permission, he opened the letter with trembling hands. He later recalled, "My joy and gratitude knew no bounds. A few days later I was wearing the tunic which I was not to doff until nearly six years later." Hitler's aimless years were over.

❧ *Three*

PURPOSE IN
WAR

Along with many other volunteers, Adolf Hitler reported to the 1st Company of the 16th Bavarian Reserve Infantry Regiment in Munich on August 16, 1914. The reserve unit was more popularly known as the List Regiment, after its original commander. At the age of twenty-five, Hitler began what he later described as "the greatest and most unforgettable time of my earthly existence." He lived at first in the Oberwiesenfeld Barracks in Munich while his regiment conducted bayonet and weapons training in the city's *Exerzierplatz* (parade ground). After about two weeks, the regiment continued its training at Lechfeld, some seventy miles west of Munich, at the confluence of the rivers Lech and Danube. There, on October 8, Hitler swore allegiance to King Ludwig III of Bavaria.

Unknown to Hitler at the time, two other members of the List Regiment would play important roles in his future. Sergeant Major Max Amann, who served as regimental clerk, would become head of Hitler's publishing enterprise and manager of the Nazi newspaper *Völkischer Beobachter (Racial Observer)*. The other, Rudolf Hess, was a student of geophysics and philosophy at Munich University who volunteered for service and received a commission at the outbreak of war. He would later be second in line to Hitler in the first years of the Third Reich.

Although the regiment's training period was only ten weeks, Hitler was impatient to get to the front and see action. He feared that the war would end before he had a chance to fight. This was a typical fear of young soldiers in the fall of 1914, but turned out to be unfounded—the war would last for more than four years.

On October 21, 1914, the List Regiment entrained for the western front. Two days later, it reached the French city of Lille, about 130 miles north of Paris. Soon it was engaged in one the fiercest and most critical battles in the early stages of the war—the first battle of Ypres.

In what came to be known as the Race to the Sea—an attempt by both Allied and German forces to secure the English Channel ports of Dunkirk and Ostend—German armies clashed with British, Belgian, and French forces near Ypres (Ieper), a Belgian town in West Flanders. After nearly 250,000 casualties, the crucial battle ended without a decisive victory for either side, as did most battles in the war. The Western Front sunk into four years of static trench warfare.

In February 1915, in a long letter to his friend, lawyer Ernst Hepp, Hitler described his first taste of conflict during a German assault on October 31, 1914:

> At last there came a ringing command: "Forward!" We swarmed out of our positions and raced across the fields to a small farm. Shrapnel was bursting left and right of us, and the English bullets came whistling through the shrapnel, but we paid no attention to them. For ten minutes we lay there, and then once again we were ordered to advance. I was right out in front, ahead of everyone in my platoon. . . . The first of our men had begun to fall. The English had set up machine guns.

Hitler and his comrades threw themselves into a ditch, splashed through a big pool of water, and ran full speed into a forest to their front.

> [I] ran as fast as I could across meadows and beet fields, jumping over trenches, hedgerows, and barbed wire entanglements. . . . There was a long trench in front of me, and in an instant I had jumped into it, and there were others in front of me, behind me, and left and right of me. . . . Under me were dead and wounded Englishmen.

When the battle ended, the ranks of the List Regiment had been reduced from 3,600 to 611 men. As Hitler put

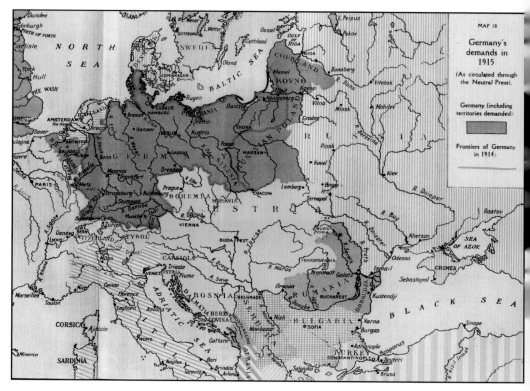

This map shows the territorial ambitions of the German Empire in 1915 during the First World War. (Library of Congress)

it later, "The volunteers of the List Regiment may not have learned to fight properly, but they knew how to die like old soldiers." Hitler, except for a sleeve ripped off by an artillery fragment, was unscathed.

Hitler seemed to enter the war convinced that Providence would not let him die or suffer crippling wounds. He spent most of the war as a *Meldegänger* (dispatch runner), a hazardous job that required him to run messages to the front from positions in the rear, often under heavy fire. Later he exaggerated his frontline experiences. He lived most of the time in comparative comfort behind the lines with periodic dangerous missions carrying messages to the front.

Hitler was a good soldier and was promoted quickly to corporal on November 3, 1914, and remained at that rank for the remainder of the war. He earned just about every award available to an enlisted soldier. In that same letter to Ernst Hepp, he wrote of his first award, "I was proposed for the Iron Cross [Second Class], the first time at Messines, then again at Wytschaete by Lieutenant Colonel Engelhardt, who was our regimental commander."

According to Engelhardt, Hitler and another orderly earned the Iron Cross for standing in front of him when he came under fire. Hitler collected four more medals before the war ended: the Cross of Military Merit, Third Class, with Swords (September 1917); the regimental diploma (May 1918); the Iron Cross, First Class (August 1918); and the Medal of Military Service, Third Class (August 1918). The Iron Cross, First Class, was the highest honor, rarely awarded to an enlisted man. Accounts vary as to why Hitler received it, but the citation itself—dated July 31, 1918, and signed by Deputy Commander Baron von Godin—reads as follows:

> As a dispatch runner, he has shown cold-blooded courage and exemplary boldness both in positional warfare and in the war of movement, and he has always volunteered to carry messages in the most difficult situations and at the risk of his life. Under conditions of great peril, when all the communication lines were cut, the untiring and fearless activity of Hitler made it possible for important messages to go through.

Corporal Hitler (front left) *with his fellow soldiers in the List Regiment in 1916.*
(National Archives)

Hitler enjoyed life as a soldier, but he was too odd to be popular among his comrades. He neither smoked nor drank and showed little interest in women, or even in taking leave. While others complained about the war dragging on and the hardships they endured, Hitler remained silent. "We all cursed him and found him intolerable," one comrade commented. "There was this white crow among us that didn't go along with us when we damned the war to hell."

Hitler never lost his fascination with or fanatical support for the war—even when things started going badly for Germany. War apparently gave him a feeling of belonging to something bigger than himself, for the first time in his life. He was convinced he was contributing to a noble cause.

Other than an occasional letter from Ernst Hepp and a former landlady in Munich, Hitler received no letters and lost all contact with his family. He generally kept to himself, spending much of his time reading. In four years of war, he read his copy of philosopher Arthur Schopenhauer's *The World as Will and Idea* until it became dog-eared. Schopenhauer's thesis is that the will alone rules and that everything else is an illusion. The idea that an individual could exert influence on the world around him intrigued Hitler. At a time when most of his colleagues and superiors were despairing at the futility of war, Hitler was becoming convinced that more will and determination was all that was needed.

Hitler did discover that even will offers little defense against the weapons of war. He was wounded twice and gassed once. His first wound came in early October 1916, during the first battle of the Somme, when an English shell struck the dispatch runners' dugout. The shell killed four of twelve runners and critically wounded six others. Hitler escaped with only a slight gash on his face from a shrapnel splinter. A few days later, on October 7, he received a more serious shrapnel wound in his left thigh while running dispatches near Baupaume. For the first time in two years, Hitler was sent to the rear for hospitalization and recuperation. He returned to his regiment in April 1917, in time to see more action in the latter stages of the battle of Arras and to take part in the third battle of Ypres that summer.

In the spring of 1918, Hitler advanced with the List

Regiment as part of the last great German offensive of the war. The Allies—mainly the British, French, and the Americans, who had recently entered the conflict—stopped this last German drive and forced the Germans steadily backward. On the night of October 13–14, the British launched a gas attack near Werwik and close to Ypres. While trying to escape from the mustard gas, Hitler was temporarily blinded and was eventually sent to a hospital to recover. While recuperating, he received word of Germany's surrender to the Allies on November 11, 1918. The news shattered him. Everything that had given his life meaning appeared to be lost in the ignominy of defeat. "And so it had all been in vain," he lamented.

Hitler blamed the German high command for Germany's defeat. As recently as late October 1918, the commanders had claimed victory was only days away. He also blamed Kaiser Wilhelm II for tolerating and consorting with Jews, who he was convinced had found a way to sabotage Germany. It was the hated Social Democrats, who controlled the Reichstag (German parliament), who insisted on suing for peace. They claimed it was in order to preserve German unity, but Hitler saw it as part of the conspiracy—Jews, he said, controlled the Social Democrats. The German fighting man, he felt, had been victim of a "stab in the back" by the high command and the Socialists (which was almost a synonym for Jews in Hitler's mind.) This betrayal, he said later, was what caused him to decide to go into politics. The war had given him a purpose, for the first time in his life, and traitors had taken it away.

In reality, Germany had suffered a military defeat in the field and was facing an imminent economic collapse. It is always difficult for military and civilian leaders to admit they led their nation to defeat, and in the turbulent months after the war—the kaiser abdicated and the government was thrown into chaos—German militarists needed a scapegoat to explain defeat. The high command, headed by General Erich von Ludendorff, helped to spread the idea that the proud army had been "stabbed in the back" by the Socialist government in Berlin. Actually, Ludendorff himself had been the one who demanded, in late September 1918, that the government ask the Allies for an immediate armistice. The Social Democrats had resisted his demands for five weeks.

Regardless of the facts, after more than four years of hardship and sacrifice, few Germans, particularly the men who had served, wanted to accept the defeat. The German army had always been invincible. The Russian czar had been overthrown because of the defeats his army suffered at German hands and the new Bolshevik Communist government had pulled Russia out of the war. That had allowed Germany to focus all its effort on the western front, and victory had seemed to be at hand. Instead, the western front had collapsed. The only explanation was treachery. In the chaotic environment of postwar Germany, many Germans accepted the myth that the Socialist government in Berlin—the "November criminals"—were responsible. Hitler became a leading perpetrator of the myth.

Hitler also alleged that the "November criminals" bore responsibility for the surrender terms inflicted upon Germany by the Allies during the negotiations held in Versailles, France, during 1919. In fact, it was again the German high command that advocated acceptance of the terms of the Treaty of Versailles. The Allies, in an attempt to prevent Germany from again becoming a powerful, belligerent nation, and to try to recapture

This map of Europe at the close of World War I shows the reduced territories of the German Empire, as well as several new European states.

some of the wealth they had expended on the war, demanded stringent concessions. Germany was required to cede large amounts of land to France, Belgium, and Poland; to assume all guilt for starting the war; to pay enormous reparations for war damages; to allow France to occupy the disputed, valuable Rhineland for fifteen years; and to limit its military forces to 100,000 men, with a ban on the production of submarines and military aircraft. In retrospect, it can be argued that it was the harshness of the Allied surrender terms that led to another war twenty years later—and the seizure of power by the former corporal Adolf Hitler.

On November 18, 1918, two days after he was released from the hospital, Hitler returned to Munich and reported to the 2nd Infantry Regiment. By March 1919, Munich was in turmoil, veering politically and experiencing political assassinations, a short-lived Soviet-style Communist government, and finally a wave of suppression by a right-wing military alliance. The political conflict was fueled by the frustration of the long-suffering German population, which wanted an end to the hardship brought on by the war. It was the ideal place for an aspiring rabble-rouser to begin a career in politics.

In January 1919, German voters elected a national assembly to write a constitution. The assembly met in Weimar, in east-central Germany, and their adopted constitution officially established a democratic federal republic in August 1919. From the start, the new Weimar

Republic suffered from economic deprivation. This was due partially to a continued Allied blockade and the burden of complying with the harsh terms of the Treaty of Versailles, as well its inability to develop wide and deep support among the citizenry.

Hitler saw the influence of Jews and Marxists everywhere in the chaos. He welcomed the chance to attend an indoctrination course at the University of Munich with radical right-leaning professors as instructors. "For me," Hitler wrote, "the value of the whole affair was that I now obtained an opportunity of meeting a few like-minded comrades with whom I could thoroughly discuss the situation of the moment."

Hitler had begun to discover that he had a talent for public speaking and worked at developing his speaking skills harder than he had worked at anything before. "I started out with the greatest enthusiasm and love," he wrote. "For all at once I was offered an opportunity of speaking before a larger audience; and the thing that I had always presumed from pure feeling without knowing it was now corroborated: I could 'speak.'"

In Bavaria, the political conflict continued even after the establishment of the Weimar Republic. Both the left-wing revolutionaries, who advocated some sort of worker's state, and the right, which tended to be aligned with the military and to accept "stabbed in the back" theories to explain the war's ignoble end, fought for control of the groundswell of discontent. Initially, it looked as though the left had the upper hand. But

Members of the Freikorps roll into Munich in an armored car with a skull painted on the grill.

Bavaria was one of the more conservative states in the German nation, and soon bands of *Freikorps* (Free Corps)—Rightist paramilitary groups made up mostly of unemployed ex-officers and ex-soldiers—roamed the streets, denouncing Jews and Marxists, and inciting revolt against the Social Democrats. Several political parties sprang up in hopes of becoming the dominant force on the radical right. One of the smallest was the *Deutsche Arbeiterpartei* (DAP), or German Workers' Party.

In September 1919, Hitler's growing prominence as a radical-Rightist lecturer led to his being entrusted with an assignment from his superiors in the army. They asked him to investigate this new German Workers' Party. At the first meeting, Hitler realized the DAP posed little threat to the army or the government. It lacked a plan of action and the money to carry out a plan if it had one. But he saw something in the tiny group that he liked, particularly in the ferocity of its opposition to the Weimar government in Berlin. The DAP had a few other definitive ideas—such as anti-Semitism—that agreed with his own. He decided to attend a few more meetings.

After several visits, Hitler joined the party. He was member number fifty-seven and soon afterward was appointed the seventh member of its Executive Committee. At the beginning of 1920, the party put Hitler in charge of propaganda. Soon he was devoting all of his

Adolf Hitler's German Workers' Party (DAP) membership card.

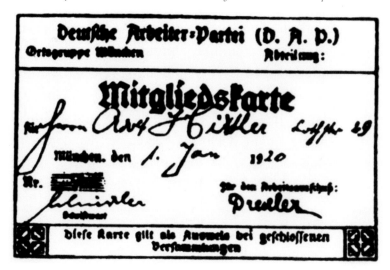

time to the tiny political party that met in beer halls and community centers. At age thirty, he now had a purpose and a podium from which to express his ideas and to see how well they went over with the beleaguered public.

✤ Four

VICTORY IN DEFEAT

What other people saw as the German Workers' Party weaknesses—tiny, poor, disorganized, unsettled on a central message—Hitler saw as an advantage. As a political nonentity himself, he understood that he would stand little chance of rising quickly to a position of influence in a more established party with a well-developed political agenda and a full leadership roster. DAP was waiting to be molded and shaped by a strong leader; Hitler was determined to be that leader.

When Hitler took charge of DAP's propaganda in January 1920, the party was a year old. It had been born in January 1919, when Anton Drexler's Committee of Independent Workmen had merged with Karl Harrer's larger group, called the Political Workers' Circle, to

Anton Drexler, one of the early leaders of the German Workers' Party. (National Archives)

become the German Workers' Party. Anton Drexler was a tall, bespectacled Munich locksmith and toolmaker whose undistinguished appearance was not made any more distinguished by the addition of a small mustache. He denounced Marxist trade unions and regarded himself as a true champion of the German working class. Karl Harrer, a shabbily dressed sports writer with a clubfoot, belonged to the Thule Society, an extremely nationalistic order devoted to racial mysticism, occultism, and anti-Semitism. Harrer served as the new party's first chairman, with Drexler as his deputy.

Hitler quickly sized up both men: "Herr Harrer . . . was certainly widely educated. But for a party leader he had one exceedingly serious drawback: he was no speaker for the masses." Nor was Drexler "very significant as a speaker." His whole nature was "feeble and uncertain," and since Drexler had never served in the army, "he lacked the only schooling which was capable of turning uncertain and soft natures into men."

"Thus both men," Hitler continued, "were not made of the stuff which would have enabled them not only to bear in their hearts fanatical faith in the victory of a movement, but also with indomitable energy and will, and if necessary with brutal ruthlessness, to sweep aside any obstacles which might stand in the path of the rising new idea." In noting the limitations of Harrer and Drexler, Hitler was actually bragging about the leadership characteristics he saw in himself. "For this," he concluded, "only beings were fitted in whom spirit and body had acquired those military virtues which can be best described as follows: swift as greyhounds, tough as leather, and hard as Krupp steel."

Harrer soon came to resent the way Hitler was dominating the party he had helped to found and resigned in protest. Drexler took over as party chairman and worked with Hitler and two other party members: Dietrich Eckart, a nationalist poet regarded as the "spiritual" godfather of the party, and Gottfried Feder, an engineer and soon to be a leading ideologist of National Socialism—to draft a DAP program.

On February 24, 1920, Hitler gave an impassioned address to an audience of almost 2,000 people in a Munich *Höfbrauhaus* (beer hall). He put forth the party's new agenda, emphasizing extreme nationalism, the nullification of the treaties that had ended World War I, anti-Semitism, German supremacy, contempt for liberal democracy, the need to expand German living space or *Lebensraum*, and advocating what was called the *Führerprinzip* (leadership principle), i.e. authoritarian rule of the party and eventually the state.

When Hitler denounced Jews and all other political parties, some in the crowd shouted in support, while others were against him. "There was often so much tumult," a police reporter in attendance wrote later, "that I believed that at any moment they would all be fighting." Two years later, in an unsigned article for the party newspaper, Hitler wrote that at the end of the meeting he felt "a wolf had been born, destined to hurl itself on the herds of seducers and deceivers of the people." Anton Drexler would technically remain the leader of the party for sixteen more months, but from that point on, Adolf Hitler was clearly in charge.

On April 1, 1920, Hitler left the army to devote all his time to the party. At his insistence, on that same day the DAP was renamed the *Nationalsozialistische Deutsche Arbeiterpartei* (NSDAP), or National Socialist German Workers' Party. In time, NSDAP became more popularly known as the Nazi Party, an acronym taken from the German words for National Socialist (*NAtionalsoZIalistische*).

Hitler instinctively realized that inflammatory oratory—a few simple ideas hammered home again and again to the masses—and a political agenda with broad appeal were essential for the small political party to attract attention and to increase membership. He also believed in the power of symbols and ritual and set to find the right symbols, pageantry, and color for the Nazi Party.

In the summer of 1920, Hitler introduced the swastika (*hakenkreuze*, hooked or crooked cross) as the party's official symbol. He incorporated the swastika into an emblem, an armband, a standard, and a flag. The flag design featured a black swastika enclosed in a white circle and set on a field of bright red. "As National Socialists, we see our program in our flag," Hitler wrote later. "In *red* we see the social idea of the movement, in

A patch showing the Nazi Party's emblem—a swastika.

white the nationalistic idea, in the *swastika* the mission of the struggle for the victory of the Aryan man." The flag would eventually become the flag of Germany's Third Reich. Hitler also introduced the use of *Heil!* as a greeting (a carryover from Schönerer's Pan-Germans). The greeting was often used with a stiff, upraised right-arm salute.

At the NSDAP congress on July 29, 1921, party members elected Hitler chairman and ceded to him dictatorial powers to mold and shape the party. He adopted the title of führer (another carryover from Schönerer), identifying himself as the supreme leader of the Nazi Party.

By the summer of 1921, the party had grown to 6,000 members, primarily on the power of Hitler's public speeches, which had begun to attract large crowds. But the ranks were not expanding fast enough to suit Hitler. He took control of the party's newspaper, the *Völkischer Beobachter.* He wanted it to more effectively spread the Nazi Party propaganda. He appointed Alfred Rosenberg, a leading proponent of the Nazi ideology, as editor, and Max Amann, the former sergeant major of the List Regiment and one of Hitler's most loyal followers, as publisher.

Hitler began to gather around him a cadre of dependable supporters. The most important were Ernst Röhm, a captain in the Reichswehr who had at one time been Hitler's commanding officer; Rudolf Hess, a former officer in the List Regiment; and Hermann Göring, a

World War I flying ace. Eventually, even Erich von Ludendorff, the supreme German commander at the end of World War I, a military hero of both the eastern and western fronts, and chief midwife of the "stabbed in the back" myth, joined the party.

In August 1921, Hitler founded the *Sturmabteilung* (Storm Detachment; hence, storm troopers), or the SA. These roughneck troopers, many of whom came from the Freikorps, wore brown uniforms with swastika armbands and marched with swastika standards. Ostensibly, they were to protect party members at mass party meetings. In truth, the mission of the SA—the soon-to-become-dreaded Brownshirts—was to instill fear in the opposition and the public through repeated acts of violence and terror. Eventually, another even-more-dreaded private army would arise from the SA—the black-shirted *Schultzstaffel* (Elite Guard), or SS, which was originally designed to be Hitler's highly disciplined personal bodyguard.

Philosophically at the core of Hitler's Nazism was a fervent nationalism and an unshakable conviction that he was able to give voice to the aspirations of the German people. Marxism, on the other hand, claimed to be international and to cut across racial and ethnic lines in its single focus on working people in conflict with the capitalists who owned factories, mines, and other busi-

Opposite: *This painting of an impassioned Hitler speaking to a small group of supporters captures some of the charisma for which Hitler quickly became known as a public speaker.* (U.S. Army Center for Military History)

nesses. Marxism also had a theoretical underpinning that could be studied and analyzed; it was put forth in works by its founder Karl Marx and dozens of other adherents, such as Vladimir Lenin, the leader of the Bolshevik Revolution that had seized power in Russia in 1917. Nazism was much more vague, more an emotional political romanticism than an articulated system. It claimed to take its authority from the mystical connection its leader had with the people.

In Italy, the Fascists, under the leadership of the former Socialist and journalist Benito Mussolini, were also fervently nationalistic and convinced they alone could speak for the Italian people. Italy had been the site of several terrible battles during the war and was still reeling from the destruction. Mussolini's party grew quickly. Hitler was aware of events to the south. He was both thrilled to see its success and jealous that Mussolini was better known.

Then, on October 22, 50,000 black-shirted Italian Fascists, under the guidance of thirty-nine-year-old Mussolini, marched on Rome and seized control of the government. "So it will be with us," Hitler reportedly stated. "We only have to have the courage to act. Without struggle, no victory!" Mussolini had shown that it was necessary to strike fast and hard. Mussolini's "March on Rome" was a model for the type of action Hitler wanted to take against the Weimar government.

By late 1923, rousing rhetoric and propaganda, the pageantry and color of standard-bearing, uniformed men on the march, and an SA-induced climate of fear and violence had ballooned the party membership to 55,000. Hitler's confidence grew as the hated Weimar Republic was growing weaker under inept leadership and the rapid inflation and stagnant economy caused primarily by the need to meet the reparation payments imposed in the peace settlement. There was active and vocal resistance to government policies from both the Left and the Right. Clearly, Germany needed a leader to restore its pride and return it to a position of prestige and power in the world community. Hitler was that man, just as Mussolini had been in Italy.

First, power would have to be seized in Bavaria. With the powerful southern state supporting him, Hitler could turn his attention to Berlin in the north. During a few hasty planning sessions in late October and early November of 1923, he put together a plot first to overthrow the Bavarian government in Munich, then to move against the central government of President Friedrich Ebert in Berlin. The plan depended on the expected support of a large army contingent stationed near Munich. Key participants in the plot included Hermann Göring, whom Hitler had made head of the SA in October 1922; Ernst Röhm, who now headed a paramilitary group of four hundred men called the German War Flag *(Deutschkriegflagge)*; and Rudolf Hess. Alfred Rosenberg and Max Erwin von Scheubner-Richter, an engineer and a member of the German diplomatic service during World War I, were the chief architects of the plot. Perhaps most importantly, General Erich von Ludendorff agreed to be at Hitler's side and to participate in the new Nazi government. Hitler was certain no soldier would fire on the former supreme commander.

The *putsch* (coup) was set to begin at a patriotic meeting to be held in the *Bürgerbräukeller*, a large beer hall in Munich, during which Bavarian state commissioner Gustav Ritter von Kahr was to deliver a speech. General Otto von Lossow, commander of the armed forces in Bavaria, and Colonel Hans von Seisser, chief of the Bavarian State Police, were to share the speaker's platform with Kahr, bringing together the three most powerful men in Bavaria. If all three were captured and then convinced to join Hitler, the putsch could succeed.

At the time, tensions were running high between the Berlin and Munich governments. Bavaria was a more conservative area than Prussia and the other parts of Germany. Communist strength and influence had grown in Berlin, and many in Munich, including the three leaders who would be on the beer hall stage, feared a Communist takeover. Hitler figured he could persuade the Bavarian leaders to march against the Weimar government.

On the evening of November 8, 1923, some 3,000 government officials gathered in the Bürgerbräukeller. While Kahr delivered his speech, six hundred SA storm troopers led by Hermann Göring surrounded the building and set up a machine gun leveled at the front entrance. Hitler, in a moment of high theater, rushed into the hall, down the darkened aisle, leaped onto a chair, fired a pistol shot at the ceiling, and announced, "The national revolution has begun. The building is occupied by six hundred heavily armed men. No one may leave the hall. The Reichswehr and police barracks have been occupied." Then he told a critical lie: "Reichswehr and police are marching on the city under the swastika banner." An eyewitness later reported that Hitler had the "expression of a madman."

Hitler then ordered Kahr, Lossow, and Seisser to accompany him to a back room. There he offered them two choices. They could fight on his side, or they could die on the spot. He would direct political affairs in Berlin's new regime, and Ludendorff would command the army. "Tomorrow will find a national government in Germany," Hitler declared, "or it will find us dead." Under duress, the three officials promised their cooperation. Hitler then announced the appointment of a new provisional government to the gathering and the crowd drifted away.

Then the unskilled plotters made a mistake. They allowed Kahr, Lossow, and Seisser to slip away unnoticed. Hitler might have even believed their promises of cooperation, although they had been given under duress. News of the putsch was brought to General Hans von Seeckt, commander of the Reichswehr in Berlin, who wired Lossow that he should quell the uprising at once or face a march on Munich from Berlin.

Later, in the early morning hours of November 9, the three Bavarian leaders publicly retracted their support for the putsch. Hitler began to foresee an unsuccessful end to his "revolution" and thought about calling it off, but Ludendorff, who was by then firmly committed, insisted on moving ahead. "The heavens will fall before the Bavarian Reichswehr turns against me," he asserted. In the meantime, about 150 men of Röhm's small group of four hundred had seized the War Ministry building—headquarters of the Bavarian Reichswehr—only to be quickly surrounded and besieged by army troops. Among the trapped Nazi rebels was the yet-unknown Heinrich Himmler, who had borne the Nazi war flag near the head of Röhm's column.

A little after 11 AM, some 3,000 Nazis assembled bearing swastika banners and war flags and began to move toward the *Marienplatz* (square) in the center of Munich. They hoped to relieve Röhm's besieged detachment with a show of force. The Nazi troopers did not know that 2,000 of their rifles had been issued without firing pins. The marching Nazis moved down the narrow street and approached another square, the *Odeonsplatz*, where one hundred police officers confronted them. Hitler ordered the police to surrender. Instead, they opened fire. In seconds, nineteen men lay dead on the pavement—sixteen Nazis and three policemen. Scheubner-Richter was shot and killed instantly. Göring received a serious wound in his upper thigh. In the midst of the fighting, several of Hitler's comrades surrounded him and hurried him off to safety at a friend's house.

General Ludendorff remained standing and marched

on through the police blockade and into the Odeonsplatz. The police turned their guns aside and let him pass. In the square, a police officer approached him and said, "Excellency, I must take you into custody." The general said, "You have your orders. I will come with you."

The police arrested Hitler two days later. The Beer Hall Putsch had ended in dismal, almost comical, failure. Hitler had failed to garner the support of the Reichswehr and the state police. Hitler said afterward, "We never thought to carry through a revolt against the army; it was with it we believed we could succeed."

The putsch was poorly planned and poorly executed. But even in failure it yielded beneficial lessons. Hitler learned never to underestimate the power of the state or

The Beer Hall Putsch defendants during their trial: (from left to right): *Heinz Pernet, Friedrich Weber, Wilhelm Frick, Hermann Kriebel, Erich Ludendorff, Adolf Hitler, Wilhelm Brückner, Ernst Röhm, Robert Wagner.* (Bayerische Staatsbibliothek, Munich)

to overestimate his own strength. Equally important, the aborted coup convinced him it was best to seek political power from within the existing political system and to work to gain the support of the masses, the army, and wealthy industrialists. Another by-product of the failure was that in a single day he went from a rabble-rouser and head of a tiny, insignificant party to the front page of every newspaper in the land. There was even international attention. Magazines and newspapers in the United States covered the story.

On February 26, 1924, Bavarian authorities brought Hitler, along with Ludendorff and a few other plotters, to trial on a charge of high treason. The trial took place in an old redbrick building used as an officers' training school in a gloomy gray suburb of Munich. Acting as his own lawyer, Hitler turned the twenty-four-day trial into a triumph of propaganda. He took full responsibility for the putsch but insisted he had done only what Kahr, Lossow, and Seisser had wanted: "This is my attitude: I would rather be hanged in a Bolshevist Germany than perish under the rule of French swords [a reference to France's occupation of German territory in January 1923]." He went on to say:

> I believe that the hour will come when the masses, who today stand in the street with our swastika, will unite with those who fired upon them. . . . One day the hour will come when the Reichswehr will stand at our side, officers and men.

That hour would not come for another nine years, but Hitler's courtroom performance impressed the German people. In closing, Hitler admonished the court: "You may pronounce us guilty a thousand times over; the goddess of the eternal court of history will smile and tear to tatters the brief of the State's attorney and the sentence of the court; for she acquits us." The court sentenced Hitler to five years in prison and acquitted General Ludendorff. Röhm was formally condemned but released at once. Göring fled to Sweden to escape trial. Hess, who had fled to Austria, returned and received a sentence of seven months.

Hitler served only nine months of his sentence at Landsberg am Lech, in a facility that was more a pleasant sanitarium than a prison. Rudolf Hess also served his sentence there. While confined, Hitler dictated the first volume of *Mein Kampf* to his fellow captive Nazis, the last of whom was Hess. The rambling, pretentious, and repetitive treatise would later become the bible of the Nazi movement. It contained his life's story, his philosophy, and his vision for the future of Germany.

Hitler's ideas reflected a sort of crude Social Darwinism. Nations, he insisted, as well as individuals, are subject to a continuing struggle for survival. Power rules and morality is folly. He warned repeatedly of the threat to the racially superior German people posed not only by the Jews but also by Marxists, liberals, and humanists or humanitarians of any kind. To regain its former great-

ness, Germany needed to wage a battle against these external forces. Germans needed to support a dictatorship that would shape a new, powerful Germany and seek *Lebensraum*—the living space denied to it by external enemies. This voluminous discourse in negativity was a slow seller when it was published, but eventually, after it became required reading in every school and home, made its author a millionaire.

On December 20, 1924, a telegram arrived at the prison at Landsberg am Lech ordering Hitler's immediate release. The Bavarian Supreme Court had granted him amnesty. During his captivity the Nazi Party had disintegrated and was near death. The speechifying corporal had had his moment of celebrity. Let him leave prison, they thought, and return to obscurity.

Opposite: *Hitler at Landsberg prison in 1924.* (Bayerische Staatsbibliothek, Munich)

FÜHRER

Hitler was released from Landsberg the day of the telegram's arrival. In the time he had been away the fortunes of the Nazi Party had dwindled. In the Reichstag elections, held a few days before his release, the Nazi candidates had won only 3 percent of the vote. On the surface it looked like a depressing state of affairs. In reality, Hitler would have wanted it no other way. The Nazi Party had only one leader; it was to be expected that it would flounder, rudderless, if he were not there.

Hitler's first move after his release was to call on Dr. Heinrich Held, the Minister President of Bavaria and leader of the Catholic Bavarian People's Party. He went to Held contritely and conceded that the Beer Hall Putsch had been a mistake. He also denounced Ludendorff, who had been making attacks on the Catholic Church, and assured Held of his intention to respect the state's authority. Held viewed Hitler's newfound humility with skepticism, but he nonetheless agreed to lift the ban on the Nazi Party and its newspaper. "The wild beast is checked," Held remarked. "We can afford to loosen the chain."

Hitler had two goals: first, solidify his control of the party by banishing all those who were not willing to accept his leadership without question; second, revitalize the Nazi Party and make it into a powerful political force. This time he would work within the constitutional framework established by the Weimar Republic.

Hitler began assembling party leaders to commence the rebuilding process. During his absence, membership had fallen off, and those who remained had split into competing groups with different ideological perspectives. Hitler understood that the first test of his leadership was to reunite these opposing factions. He began with a spirited speech to some 3,000 at Munich's Bürgerbräukeller on February 27, 1925. It was a capacity crowd; 2,000 people were turned away.

Max Amann introduced Hitler, who focused the first part of his speech on the party's opposition to Marxism and the Jew, which he saw as one monolithic force. "Fight Marxism and Judaism not according to middle-class standards," he urged, "but over corpses!"

Toward the end of the two-hour speech, he turned the focus to a more immediate problem. It was necessary for the Nazi Party to have a leader. No challenges to his total

A dramatic and fiery Hitler speaks to a crowd of Nazi supporters. (Library of Congress)

control would be tolerated. He turned to the party leaders seated at nearby tables and said, "This is an absolutely new beginning. You must forget your personal quarrels. If you will not, I shall start the party alone, without you." In the future, Germany would be ruled by a dictator with an elite corps of assistant leaders. "Every man will have advisers to help him," he said, "but the decision will be made by one man."

Max Amann stepped forward and shouted: "The wrangling must stop! Everyone for Hitler!" People leapt up and cheered; shouts of "Heil Hitler!" filled the hall. In a scant two hours, Hitler had begun the process of reuniting the party and reestablishing the *Führerprinzip* (leadership principle).

There was a price to be paid for his fiery rhetoric,

however. What had seemed like a great step forward for the Nazi Party on the night of February 27 was a negative by the morning of February 28 when Bavarian officials, outraged at Hitler's inflammatory rhetoric, prohibited him from speaking in public in Bavaria. The ban, which soon spread to other German states, lasted until May 1927 in Bavaria and September 1928 in Prussia. This prohibition presented a severe handicap to Hitler, whose greatest asset was his oratorical power.

Also on February 28, 1925, Friedrich Ebert, the first president of the Weimar Republic, died. In the presidential elections held in March, Erich von Ludendorff, who was still the Nazi-backed candidate, won only 211,000 of 27 million votes cast. In a runoff election in April 1925, the Nazis supported Field Marshal Paul von Hindenburg, a last-minute candidate brought in by a party of German nationalists aligned with wealthy industrialists. Hitler supported Hindenburg because "in him our people's will for liberty is coupled with the righteousness and honesty of the greatest models in our history." Hindenburg eked out a narrow victory, but Hitler and the Nazis had little reason to rejoice. President Hindenburg—a venerated figure of the old Army, who was a stanch monarchist, conservative, and nationalist—lent an air of stability to the Weimar government and seemed to begin the process of reconciling conservative, powerful Germans to the Weimar regime. A stable Germany was not prone to listen to a radical such as Hitler. Over the next few years the Nazi message, which had seemed to strike a chord in the turbulent months after World War I, found fewer adherents. The political climate had shifted. It seemed, for a short while, that political stability under the democratic Weimar constitution might survive.

The relative stability in Germany in the last half of the 1920s was primarily due to improving economic conditions. The Dawes Plan, pushed by the United States and named after the American head of the Reparations Committee of the Allied Nations, had helped Germany meet its reparation payments without totally devastating the country's budget. Before the plan, Germany's currency had been rendered worthless by runaway inflation set off by the government printing cash to make the crushing payments.

International events were also unfavorable to Nazi prosperity. Postwar disputes over territory were settled amicably. Germany was allowed entry into the League of Nations in September 1926. More Germans had jobs, homes, food, and hope for the future. A war-weary people, they were sick of political turmoil and hoped for a stable future.

In the meantime, Hitler had many things to do to strengthen the tiny Nazi party and his control of it. In April 1925, the SS *(Schutzstaffel)*, Hitler's elite guard, was created. Originally staffed by men of the *Stosstrupp* (shock troop), assault troops who were used to guard the stages where Hitler gave his speeches, the SS would soon emerge as the Nazi Party's chief police arm. On the last

Nazi propagandist Joseph Goebbels. (National Archives)

day of the month, Hitler relinquished his Austrian citizenship.

For a while, the biggest thorns in Hitler's side were Gregor and Otto Strasser. Gregor, the elder brother, was a huge, burly, round-faced former army lieutenant who had earned the Iron Cross, First and Second Classes. Otto Strasser, more intellectual than his brother, founded a weekly newspaper, the *Berliner Arbeiterzeitung* (Berlin Worker's Paper). He hired Joseph Goebbels, a small, thin-faced, sharp-featured propagandist who suffered from a deformed foot, as an editor. The Strasser brothers were influential in Berlin. They advocated a more worker-based philosophy than did Hitler, who had begun the process of quietly seeking support from wealthy capitalists. This split in ideology, between the more capitalistic, nationalistic Hitler and the more anticapitalist Strasser brothers, would continue for some time.

Hitler spent much of the summer of 1925 in the small Bavarian mountain village of Berchtesgaden, where he established an auxiliary party headquarters. There he finished writing the first volume of *Mein Kampf*. The book was unofficially issued on July 18, 1925, and officially published the following December 8. Because of the ban on public speaking, Hitler had extra time available to him. He spent it trying to strengthen the party's apparatus. He reinstated Alfred Rosenberg as editor of the *Völkischer Beobachter* and rejected Ernst Röhm's demands for full authority over the SA. He planned to revitalize it as an instrument of his own

The picturesque Bavarian village of Berchtesgaden, where Hitler would eventually build a mountain retreat. (Library of Congress)

authority. This was the beginning of a long period of tension and conflict with Röhm.

In January 1926, Strasser organized a two-day meeting of party leaders in Hannover, Germany, to draft a new party program. Hitler refused to go and sent Gottfried Feder to represent him. After a round of heated arguments, Feder said, "Neither Hitler nor I will accept this program." Feder then hastened back to Munich and warned Hitler of an open revolt in the party. Hitler called for his own meeting of party leaders at Bamberg on February 14 to resolve the differences between northern and southern district leaders.

At the February meeting, southern leaders loyal to Hitler greatly outnumbered those from the north. From the moment he took the speaker's rostrum, he dominated the proceedings. He spoke for two hours and surprised the northern leaders by not attacking the two principal northern spokesmen, Gregor Strasser and Joseph Goebbels, but instead spoke of his authority as the führer of the party. He forbade any further parliamentarian debates, democratic procedures, and splinter groups. The original party program, Hitler told them, "was the foundation of our religion, our ideology. To tamper with it would [constitute] treason to those who died believing in our idea." Accept him as the absolute leader—give him their total allegiance—or find another führer. Strasser knew he was beaten and made only a brief response. Hitler's oratory had again carried the day, but any final resolution to the philosophical differences between Strasser and Hitler was deferred.

After this meeting, the always-opportunistic Goebbels realized Hitler would be the ultimate victor and began to gradually shift his allegiance. Hitler appointed him *Gauleiter* (District Leader) of Berlin on December 1, 1926.

That month, Hitler published the second volume of *Mein Kampf.* It had two themes: Jews stand at the heart of all the world's problems, and all great nations need to expand their living space. Hitler also touched on the issue of the former German territory of South Tyrol, which had been ceded to Italy by the Treaty of St. Germain. He also acknowledged the growing economic power of the United States. Publication of the second

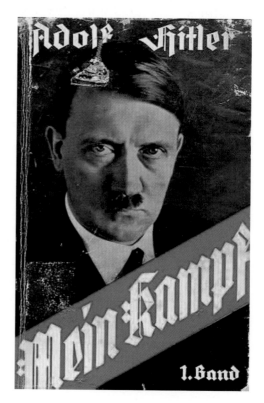

Hitler's best-selling book, Mein Kampf (My Struggle), *combined his political ideology of National Socialism with elements of his life story.*

volume coincided with the January 1927 removal of the speaking ban against him in Saxony, followed in March by Bavaria. Goebbels provided Hitler with an additional conduit to the masses when he began to publish his own newspaper, *Der Angriff* (The Assault), in July 1927.

On August 19–21, 1927, the Nazis held their second *Parteitag* (Party Day) rally in Nuremberg. Some 30,000 Brownshirts marched through the streets of the city that was to become the showplace of Nazism. The first Party Day rally had been held a year earlier in Weimar on July 3–4, with an attendance of 7,000–8,000, including 3,600 SA and 116 SS men. The Nuremberg rally demonstrated a marked increase in party membership over the past year, but the numbers still fell short of Hitler's expectations. The Reichstag elections of May 20, 1928, which gave only 12 of 491 seats and 2.5 percent of the vote to the Nazi Party, also disappointed him. Two of the twelve seats went to a pair of Hitler's favored disciples— Hermann Göring, who had returned from exile, and Joseph Goebbels. In *Der Angriff*, Goebbels declared jubilantly, "We are going into the Reichstag . . . like the wolf into the sheepflock."

After eight years of struggle, Hitler was still far removed from power. But at the start of 1929, world conditions began to work in his favor. He began the year by appointing Heinrich Himmler, a bespectacled former chicken farmer, as *Reichsführer-SS* (Reich SS Leader) on January 6. Himmler, deceptively meek in appearance, had once served as Gregor Strasser's adjutant and

Heinrich Himmler, head of the SS. (Library of Congress)

later as his secretary. Hitler wanted to promote Himmler and the SS as a counter to the increasingly rowdy and often scandalous SA. He wanted a more reliable security force, out of Röhm's control, with which he could dominate the party and later the nation. It would take Himmler several years to build such a force, but Hitler had found the right man for the job.

On June 7, 1929, the Young Plan—which called for German reparation payments to be set at $26.35 billion and to continue all the way until 1988—was signed in Paris. Most Germans on the right saw the Young Plan as an insult to national honor. Hitler aligned himself with Alfred Hugenberg, a vocal German nationalist, in opposition. The wealthy Hugenberg owned a vast network of news agencies and newspapers, as well as a controlling interest in the big UFA film company, and was the chairman of the *Deutschnationale Volkspartei* (German Nationalist People's Party). In addition to his own wealth, he had the financial support of industrial interests. To advance their special interests, these men of power and influence lacked only a charismatic figure to agitate across the land and rouse the masses.

Although he was a political rival, Hugenberg shared many of Hitler's intolerant opinions. He was usually vigilant about keeping his party from forming alliances with other groups that might compromise its message, or his power, but Hitler made the tactical decision to align the Nazis with the media mogul's vast propaganda machine. He collaborated with Hugenberg to draft a "Law against the Enslavement of the German People," which repudiated Germany's responsibility for World War I, demanded the end of reparations, and called for the indictment of high government officials for treason if they agreed to new financial commitments. Hitler knew the law had no chance to be passed in the Social Democrat-controlled Reichstag. However, he saw the law's defeat as the best possible outcome for the Nazis. Afterward he would be able to argue it was the only party dedicated to restoring honor and dignity to Germany. Their measure was soundly defeated in the Reichstag. President Hindenburg signed the Young Plan on March 13, 1930.

The defeat of the "Law against the Enslavement of the

German People" was a propaganda victory for the Nazis. Hitler had become a familiar figure thanks to Hugenberg's money and the exposure provided by his media outlets. More important, Hitler had caught the eye of other supportive purse holders in the world of heavy industry and high finance.

On September 5, 1929, Hitler moved from his modest quarters on Thierschstrasse to an opulent nine-room apartment covering the entire second floor at Prinzregentenplatz 16, on one of Munich's more fashionable streets. He also bought a new Mercedes-Benz touring car, added a second secretary and two or three servants to his staff, and purchased the Haus Wachenfeld, a country villa in the Bavarian Alps.

These were heady days for Hitler, who was now seen more frequently about town, occasionally in the company of his niece, Geli Rabaul. The daughter of Hitler's half sister Angela, Geli was a twenty-one-year-old blue-eyed beauty. She had come to Munich to study medicine and occupied a room in Hitler's new flat. The attention he lavished on his attractive niece soon became an item of gossip. In later times, Hitler would recall these days:

> In the evening I would put on a dinner jacket or tails to go to the opera. We made excursions by car. . . . My super-charged Mercedes was a joy to all. Afterwards, we would prolong the evening in the company of the actors. . . . From all points of view, those were marvelous days.

Hitler's tragic niece and mistress, Geli Rabaul.

Hitler usually ate in one of his favorite cafes. A teetotaler and vegetarian, he also detested tobacco smoke and forbade smoking around him. Always with aides and bodyguards, he usually dominated the table talk, expounding on his theories or the superiority of Wagnerian opera or other aesthetic concerns.

Hitler apparently thought he was offering Geli everything a young girl from the provinces should want, but she soon grew restless and bored under his control. She told a few of Hitler's aides that she wanted to marry someone her age and maybe even return home. Hitler refused to grant her any freedom. While the exact nature of their relationship is impossible to determine, Hitler was clearly fixated on his half niece. When he could not be with her, he arranged to have her watched. He said it was for her protection, but clearly he did not want her to flee.

Geli grew increasingly and obviously frustrated and depressed. Finally, apparently convinced she would never be free from Hitler's control, and possibly despondent over a young man she wanted to marry, she committed suicide in Hitler's apartment. Hitler was in Nuremberg when she died. Hitler's associates were able to keep Geli's suicide from becoming a major scandal.

Hitler had met Eva Braun in early October 1929, two years before Geli's death. She was a vibrant seventeen-year-old who worked in the photo shop of Heinrich Hoffman, the official photographer to Hitler and the Nazi Party. Blond, tall, slim, and athletic, Eva was, as one of her teachers recalled, "intelligent and quick to seize

Eva Braun, Hitler's lifelong companion and eventual wife. (Courtesy of the Granger Collection.)

the essential aspects of a subject, and she was capable of independent thought." Hoffman introduced his young employee to Hitler, who began to come by the shop frequently with flowers and candy for "my lovely siren from Hoffman's." Over the next fifteen years she would gradually become his companion, finally marrying him only moments before their mutual suicide in 1945.

In mid-October of 1929, the U.S. stock market crashed, precipitating a worldwide financial crisis that led to the decade-long Great Depression. In the second half of the 1920s, when most parts of the world economy had been growing, Germany had been able to make its reparations payments in a timely manner and to begin an economic recovery financed primarily by foreign loans. Before the war, the German economy had been the second largest in the world, behind the United States. The loans had reinvigorated the economy but now Germany was faced with imminent bankruptcy. The number of Germans out of work rose from 1.6 million in 1929 to 6.12 million by 1932. Hitler saw the Depression as a golden opportunity.

Hitler was now ready to apply the lessons he had learned while waging his campaign with Alfred Hugenberg against the Young Plan. He knew little about economics and finance, but he knew that vast sums of money would be needed. "In the summer of 1931," recalled Nazi publicist and press chief Otto Dietrich, "the Führer suddenly decided to concentrate systematically on cultivating the influential industrial magnates."

Hitler enlisted the aid of Walther Funk, his personal economics adviser and a former journalist who enjoyed the confidence of numerous big industrialists. Funk succeeded in persuading large companies to donate money that they had once sent to the more reputable political parties.

On September 14, 1931, the Nazi Party won 18 percent of the vote and 107 of 577 seats in the Reichstag in the general elections, making it Germany's second-strongest party. Five months later, on February 25, 1932, Adolf Hitler became a German citizen. He decided to run for the presidency in March but was defeated by Hindenburg in a runoff election, garnering 13.4 million votes to the popular war hero's 19.4 million. After the loss, a district leader found his disappointed führer in the remotest room of the party's hotel suite: Hitler, "alone, back bent, looking tired and morose, sat at a round table slowly sipping his vegetable soup."

In the general elections of July 31, 1932, the Nazis won 230 of 608 seats in the Reichstag to become Germany's strongest party. During the next two weeks, General Kurt von Schleicher, chief of the Ministerial Bureau of the Reichswehr Ministry and a principal confidant of President Hindenburg, attempted to broker a deal behind the scenes to appoint Hitler as German chancellor. (In the Weimar government, the chancellor was responsible for running the government and setting policy while the president was more of a symbolic office.) But Hindenburg quashed the idea, sneering that he

Hitler bows to German president Paul von Hindenburg. (Courtesy of the Granger Collection.)

would not appoint a "Bohemian corporal" as chancellor.

On August 13, Hitler met with Hindenburg in Berlin. The president told him that neither conscience nor sense of duty would permit him "to transfer the whole authority of government to a single party, especially to a party that was biased against people who had different views from their own." Instead, the president offered the former corporal the vice chancellorship. Hitler, shrewdly, declined. Hindenburg ended the audience, commenting, "We are both old comrades and we want to remain so, since the course of events may bring us together again later on."

Six
SEIZURE OF POWER

At the end of 1932, Hitler found that his road to power was blocked by General Kurt von Schleicher, who had convinced Hindenburg to appoint Franz von Papen chancellor the previous June. But when Papen was unable to win a vote of support from the Reichstag in November, an embarrassed and angry Hindenburg forced Schleicher to take the office on December 3, 1932.

As chancellor, Schleicher, who had no political party support, attempted to unite the Reichswehr and trade unions against the Nazis while, at the same time, he secretly negotiated with Hitler for a cabinet position in any future National Socialist government. Apparently, Schleicher hoped to use the Nazis to gain power himself. Hitler refused to offer Schleicher a position.

Schleicher made other attempts to divide the NSDAP, primarily by making overtures to Gregor Strasser, who still represented the left wing of party, comprised mostly of workers. Hitler was able to deflect each of Schleicher's moves. Meanwhile, the Nazis grew stronger. After Hitler again rejected the vice chancellory, Hindenburg bowed to the reality of Hitler's political strength. On January 30, 1933, acting in full accord with the constitution of the Weimar Republic, he appointed Adolf Hitler chancellor of Germany.

Six hours later, Hitler stood in the window of the chancellery and watched 25,000 members of the SA and

SA men march through the Brandenburg Gate after the appointment of Hitler as chancellor of Germany on January 30, 1933. (Courtesy of Bildarchiv Preussischer Kulturbesitz / Art Resource, NY.)

SS march out of Berlin's *Tiergarten* (zoological garden), down the Wilhelmstrasse, and through the Brandenburg Gate in a torchlight parade. He was heard to whisper, "No power on earth will ever get me out of here alive." In a letter written on February 2, 1930, he had predicted "with almost clairvoyant certainty" that "the victory of our movement will take place . . . at the most in two and a half to three years."

On February 1, General Erich von Ludendorff, who had long since broken with Hitler, sent a prophetic telegram to Hindenburg:

> By appointing Hitler Chancellor of the Reich, you have handed over our sacred German Fatherland to one of the greatest demagogues of all time. I prophesy to you that this evil man will plunge our Reich into the abyss and will inflict immeasurable woe on our nation. Future generations will curse you in your grave for this action.

It is unlikely that the eighty-five-year-old Hindenburg, who was nearing senility, ever read the telegram. In all probability, his aides never delivered it to him.

On the night of February 10, Hitler delivered his first radio broadcast to the nation as chancellor, standing before an enthusiastic audience in Berlin. In his speech, he chronicled his fourteen years of struggle and pledged to stamp out Marxism with the help of the *Volk* (people). He promised a program "of national resurrection in all areas of life," which, with the help of the people, would produce "the new German kingdom of greatness and power and glory and justice. Amen." All too soon, the Christian approbation of "Amen" would give way to affirmations of "Sieg Heil!"

Rapid changes were in store for Germany. The first occurred at about ten o'clock on the evening of February 27, 1933, when a Berlin resident alerted the police to a fire in the dome of the Reichstag building. The fire destroyed the structure. Allegedly set by a Dutch Communist named Marinus van der Lubbe, many suspect that the Nazis started the fire themselves. The issue remains unresolved. What is known is that Hitler used the blaze to turn public opinion against the Communists—who held one hundred seats in the Reichstag— and other rivals. He persuaded President Hindenburg to enact emergency decrees suspending the freedom of speech and press. British reporter Douglas Reed described the effects:

> When Germany awoke, a man's home was no longer his castle. He could be seized by private individuals, could claim no protection from the police, could be indefinitely detained without preferment of charge; his property could be seized, his verbal and written communications overheard and perused; he no longer had the right to foregather with his fellow countrymen, and his newspapers might no longer freely express their opinions.

In the immediate aftermath of the Reichstag fire, the Nazis—spearheaded by the SA—arrested thousands of

Communists. The SA, which had already gained a reputation for bloodletting and violence, lived up to its
image. One storm trooper reported:

> We were prepared; we knew the intentions of our
> enemies. I had put together a small "mobile squad" of
> my storm [company] from the most daring of the
> daring. We lay in wait night after night. Who was
> going to strike the first blow? And then it came. The
> beacon in Berlin, signs of fire all over the country.
> Finally the relief of the order: "Go to it!" And we went
> to it! It was not just about the purely human "you or
> me," "you or us," it was about wiping the lecherous
> grin off the hideous, murderous faces of the
> Bolsheviks for all time, and protecting Germany
> from the bloody terror of unrestrained hordes.

Actually, it was the SA troopers themselves who
unleashed "the bloody terror of unrestrained hordes,"
and the blood of their victims flowed in the streets and
alleys of German cities all across the land. The emergency
decrees, augmented by the SA wave of terror, cleared the
way for the Nazis to seize control. On March 5, 1933, the
Nazis won 288 of the 647 seats in the Reichstag elections. Despite the arrest or flight from the country of
many of its candidates, the Communist Party won eighty-
one seats, but they would not be allowed to serve. Most
were arrested as soon as the police could find them. By
removing eighty-one Communist seats, the Nazis
achieved a 288-278 seat majority.

With his power strengthened, Hitler began to select

Nazi party leadership: (from left to right) *Adolf Hitler, Hermann Göring, Joseph Goebbels, and Rudolf Hess.* (National Archives)

his favorites for key appointments. The portly Hermann Göring, who had been elected president of the Reichstag after the November 1932 elections, was given a number of important posts. Hitler also named him as next in line, his immediate successor. Hitler made Himmler police president of Munich on March 9, designated Goebbels Reich Minister for Public Enlightenment on March 13, and named Dr. Hjalmar Schacht president of the Reichsbank on March 16. The next day, he formed the *Leibstandarte-SS Adolf Hitler* (SS Bodyguard Regiment Adolf Hitler) under command of Josef (Sepp) Dietrich, a tough, brawny, and brutal lieutenant general in the SS, who was totally devoted to his führer. On March 20, Himmler announced to the press that "a concentration camp for political prisoners" would be

The formidable SA parades through the streets, each soldier giving the Nazi salute as he passes Hitler. (Library of Congress)

opened at Dachau, twelve miles north of Munich.

On March 23, the Nazis proposed new legislation known as the Enabling Bill, a sweeping measure empowering the new government to enact laws without the approval of the Reichstag. It would require an alteration to the Weimar Constitution by a majority vote of two-thirds, ninety votes of which would have to come from outside the NSDAP. It took a day for the first law submitted to the Nazi-controlled Reichstag to pass by a vote of 441 to 94. The excess votes were primarily the result of the intimidating presence of the SA lined up in the Kroll Opera House, which was the temporary home of the Reichstag.

The Enabling Law granted Hitler absolute powers for a period of four years. It would be renewed in 1937 and made perpetual in 1943. However, Hitler realized he had work to do before he could claim permanent control as Germany's dictator. He began by promulgating a series of laws designed to create a highly centralized one-party Reich. This process was called *Gleichschaltung* (coordination), and it proceeded along two related lines aimed at synchronizing all government institutions and mobilizing all Germans for the National Socialist cause. Through Gleichschaltung, Hitler created Germany's Third Reich, which he predicted would last for a thousand years.

On March 31, the new Reichstag passed the first unification law, called the Temporary Law for the Coordination of the States with the Reich, which stripped individual states of all sovereign powers and transferred all decisions to the Reich minister of the interior, Wilhelm Frick. The next day, April 1, Hitler ordered a boycott of Jewish businesses. SA troopers took up position in front of Jewish shops to bar entry. The boycott had little to do with the "unification" process but was a harbinger of Hitler's coming war against the Jews. That same day, Göring appointed Himmler as head of the Gestapo *(Geheime Staatspolizei,* or secret state police)—a secret police dedicated to maintaining the Nazi regime. Later in April, special courts were established to try political offenses, including a People's Court in Berlin for trials of high treason.

In May 1933, Hitler dissolved all labor unions and prohibited strikes throughout Germany. Joseph Goebbels, as propaganda minister, encouraged students across the land to purge libraries of "un-German" books. On the night of May 11, SA and SS bands played for a torchlight parade in the city's center while students tossed some 20,000 books into a huge bonfire. Included among them were the works of Jews, liberals, and noncompliant intellectuals such as Thomas Mann, Albert Einstein, Sigmund Freud, Marcel Proust, and H. G. Wells.

In June and July, Hitler outlawed all political parties except the Nazi Party and made all unions subservient, eventually bringing them together under Dr. Robert Ley's *Deutsche Arbeitsfront* (German Labor Front). In

A crowd of supporters gives the Nazi salute during the infamous book burning of May 11, 1933 in Berlin. (National Archives)

a parallel attack on the independence of professions, Hitler dissolved the old professional bodies and reorganized them into "fronts" or "academies." In a far-reaching move in September, the news and entertainment media—radio, music, journalism, and drama—were brought under the control of Joseph Goebbels in his newly formed Reich Chamber of Culture. For the time being, Gleichschaltung exempted industry and the armed forces from reorganization, but it devastated the other political, social, and cultural institutions of Germany. It succeeded in reducing class and professional differences, but at an enormous cost to individual rights.

In October 1933, the League of Nations refused Hitler's demands to allow Germany to be released from the limitations on its military and armament supplies agreed upon in 1919. Hitler had always considered the league to be a mere extension of the Allied victors of World War I. He used the refusal to announce Germany's withdrawal from disarmament talks and pulled out of the international body. Germany began a program of accelerated rearmament. His countrymen were behind Hitler; the Nazis won 95.2 percent of the vote in new Reichstag elections held on November 12, 1933.

In order to buy time to build up the armed forces for a future war, Hitler signed a ten-year nonaggression pact with neighboring Poland on January 26, 1934. On January 30, the first anniversary of Hitler's appointment as chancellor, he could look back at a highly productive year. His path to total control, however, remained blocked by three obstacles, all relating to the tensions created by the powerful and undisciplined SA. The SA leaders and those in the party aligned with it—principally Gregor Strasser and Ernst Röhm—continued to call impatiently for the "second revolution." This new stage of the Nazi takeover was supposed to break up many of the larger industries and financial institutions and to spread the wealth among the workers. Hitler knew this would cost him critical corporate support and had no intention of delivering on this promise. He was concerned about the imperial greatness of a militant Germany, not the social-ist dreams of the average worker. Another related prob-lem was the intense rivalry between the SA and the German army. The army was the bastion of the older conservatives, with its aristocratic and upper-middle-class officer corps that looked with disdain at the Brownshirts. Finally, the question of who would succeed President Paul von Hindenburg, who was near death that spring, was a nagging problem that would have to be taken care of soon. Röhm had made his desire for the job clear.

After the failure of the Beer Hall Putsch in 1923, Ernst Röhm had been tried and convicted of treasonable acts. He was also dismissed from the army. Shortly afterward, he went abroad to work as a military instructor in Bo-livia. Soldiering was his life. "From my childhood," he began his memoirs, entitled *The Story of a Traitor*, "I had only one thought and wish—to be a soldier." He was a very good one. In January 1931, Hitler had recalled

Röhm and reinstated him as head of the SA, which then numbered about 70,000 men. By the end of 1931, Röhm had more than doubled the size of the SA, and by the start of 1934, it had almost 4.5 million members.

During Hitler's rise to power, the SA—an army of street fighters, gangsters, and toughs—played a critical role in winning the battle of the streets against the Communists. Hitler rewarded Röhm by appointing him to the Reich Cabinet. But Hitler no longer needed the SA, whose brutal and scandalous behavior, including public displays of brawling, drinking, and indiscreet remarks, as well as Röhm's rumored homosexuality, was beginning to create controversy. Military leaders were also alarmed at Röhm's resolve to absorb the SA into the regular army with himself at the head of the combined force.

As SA chief of staff, Reich minister without portfolio, and minister of the Bavarian state government, Röhm held strong positions in the Third Reich. He apparently thought he was too powerful to be at risk. But Röhm underestimated the number of formidable foes, both inside the army and within the party, aligned against him and overestimated his support.

In April 1934, Hitler met with top military leaders. He needed to assure them that he would take care of Röhm and that he had no intention of displacing them from the military leadership. He was already thinking long term in his plans to go to war. He granted the generals two major concessions: he would end Röhm's challenge to their authority, and he would maintain the traditional form of the German military. In return, the military commanders pledged their allegiance. This agreement also pleased the major industrialists, who had been nervous about the calls for a second revolution.

On June 4, 1934, Hitler summoned Röhm to a meeting. The two men conferred for five hours. Hitler, who still expressed fondness for his old comrade, pleaded with him. "Forget the idea of a second revolution," Hitler urged. "Believe in me. Don't cause any trouble." He assured Röhm he had no intentions of dissolving the SA, to which he felt deeply indebted, but he did order the SA to go on leave for the month of July. While on leave, the

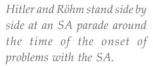

Hitler and Röhm stand side by side at an SA parade around the time of the onset of problems with the SA.

storm troopers were not to wear uniforms. The two men agreed to meet for further discussions on July 1 at Bad Wiessee, a popular resort spa north of Munich.

In the meantime, Hitler flew to Venice on June 14 for his first meeting with Italian dictator Benito Mussolini, or "Il Duce" ("The Leader"), as he was popularly known. Mussolini greeted Hitler at Venice's Lido airport, resplendently garbed in a uniform of black shirt, jackboots, and gold braid. Hitler wore an old felt hat and a rumpled trench coat over a blue serge suit. He appeared nervous in the face of a contingent of Italian troops in full dress. Mussolini seemed more amused than impressed by his German counterpart and pressed Hitler on the subject of Austrian autonomy. Italy and Austria had long dueled over control of Trieste and other areas near their common border, and Mussolini wanted Hitler to acknowledge Italy's claim. Il Duce did not hesitate to comment on the internal situation in Germany. He advised Hitler to restrain the left wing of the Nazi Party. Hitler returned to Berlin convinced that he had left "a strong impression" behind with the Italians.

On June 26, Himmler alerted all SS and SD (SD stands for *Sicherheitsdienst*, or Security Service, the intelligence branch of the SS then under the command of Reinhard Heydrich) leaders of the "impending revolt of the SA under Röhm." Although there was no real evidence that Röhm was planning a coup against Hitler, the warning succeeded in raising tensions and apparently convinced Hitler the threat was accurate. Two days later,

Hitler left Berlin, so as to "present an outward impression of absolute calm and to give no warning to the traitors." On June 29, Göring ordered his Berlin units on full alert. That evening, Hitler flew to Munich and proceeded at about 4 AM to Nazi headquarters in the Brown House at Briennerstrasse 45. What came to be known as the "Night of the Long Knives" was set to begin.

Early on Saturday morning, June 30, Hitler, along with Goebbels and several others close to the führer, left Munich and drove to Bad Wiessee in a column of cars filled with SS enforcers. When they arrived at the Pension Hanselbauer, the private hotel where Röhm and other SA officers were staying, Hitler, riding whip in hand, went directly to Röhm's room and demanded entry. Once inside, he blurted, "Röhm, you're under arrest!" Concurrently, SS men kicked down the door of a nearby room and shot and killed another SA officer and his male bedmate on the spot. Röhm and several other SA leaders were herded into waiting automobiles and driven to Munich's Stadelheim Prison.

Meanwhile, at the Brown House, Rudolf Hess and a cordon of SS troops were busy seizing surprised and bewildered SA officers as they arrived for the July 1 meeting with Hitler. They, too, were sent to Stadelheim Prison, where some seven hundred to eight hundred men of Sepp Dietrich's SS Leibstandarte had been brought in to man firing squads. When Hitler returned to the Brown House, he telephoned Göring in Berlin and announced the code word *Kolibri* (hummingbird). Under the direction of the Göring-Himmler-Heydrich triumvirate, more than 150 top SA leaders had already been arrested and imprisoned in a coal cellar at the Lichterfelde Cadet School Barracks. After Hitler's call, the executions commenced.

In Berlin, SS assassins led off their SA victims four at a time and shot them in front of a wall in the courtyard. SS officers finished off victims who lay screaming and writhing on the ground with a single shot to the head. Firing squads were changed often because the executioners became visibly upset. The killing continued throughout Saturday and Sunday, and the list of victims was extended beyond just SA leaders. Gregor Strasser was seized and shot in his cell; former chancellor General Kurt von Schleicher—who felt only contempt for Röhm—and his wife were killed in their home. Hitler was settling old scores.

On Monday, July 2, on Hitler's orders, Röhm's captors placed a revolver with one bullet in his cell and ordered him to use it within ten minutes. Röhm refused. "If Adolf wants to kill me," he said, "let him do the dirty work himself." After ten minutes, two guards entered Röhm's cell and retrieved the revolver. Theodor Eicke, commandant of the Dachau concentration camp, and his aide, Michael Lippert, then entered the cell and pumped bullets into the bare-chested Röhm. His body was buried in the courtyard in an unknown location.

In a terse statement, Hitler later explained, "The former Chief of Staff Röhm was given the opportunity to draw the consequences of his treacherous behavior. He did not do so and was thereupon shot." Röhm had failed to grasp the risk he took by threatening Hitler's leadership and paid dearly for it. The precise number of Hitler's adversaries who died during the Night of the Long Knives remains uncertain, but some estimates put the death toll as high as 2,000.

On July 13, Hitler addressed the Reichstag. He laid the blame for the bloodbath on Röhm and others, and portrayed himself as the savior of the German people. "Let the nation know that its existence—which depends on its internal order and security—cannot be threatened with impunity by anyone!" he concluded.

The last obstacle to absolute power was removed when President Hindenburg died on August 2, 1934. Within an hour, Hitler issued a statement combining the office of president with that of chancellor. Hitler was now head of the state and supreme commander of the armed forces—in short, dictator of Germany. On August 19, German citizens voted to affirm Hitler's new powers with 89.93 percent of 45.5 million votes cast. In September, at the party rally in Nuremburg, Hitler declared that the revolution had achieved its objective and had come to an end: "In the next thousand years there will be no other revolution."

Seven

LEBENSRAUM

The consolidation of the chancellorship and the presidency, combined with the sweeping changes of Gleischaltung, brought what Hitler called a New Order to Germany. By the start of 1935, the New Order had totally rearranged German life to conform with Hitler's *Weltanschaung* (world view). He had replaced the government with a Nazi administration ruled from the top down by himself and his appointees. The New Order promised to bring prosperity to the German people and restore Germany to worldwide prominence. As dictator, Hitler was now positioned to act on the two recurring themes of *Mein Kampf*—the pursuit of *Lebensraum* (living space), and a solution to the "Jewish question," i.e., the removal of all Jews from Germany.

Hitler's quest for living space began with the new year when the citizens of the Saarland, a region of valuable mines along the Saar River, voted to return to Germany. A provision of the Treaty of Versailles allowed the Saar inhabitants to vote, after fifteen years, on whether they wanted to maintain the status quo, become part of France, or return to Germany. The result of the plebiscite of mostly German voters on January 13 was predictable, and the Saarland reverted to the Third Reich.

Hitler used its return for propaganda purposes. On March 1, the day of the district's formal incorporation, he spoke in Saarbrücken, the Saar capital. He hoped the settlement of the Saar issue meant "relations between Germany and France had improved once and for all. Just as we want peace, so we must hope that our great neighboring people is also willing and ready to seek peace with us." Hitler's words intentionally misrepresented his thoughts. Peace was the last thing he wanted, but he needed time to build up the military.

Disarmament talks in Geneva had stagnated since Hitler had withdrawn from both the talks and the League of Nations in October 1933. But the Western powers— chiefly Great Britain, France, and Italy—continued to pressure Hitler for an arms agreement. At the same time, Britain and France took measures to safeguard their own borders. On March 4, Britain announced plans for increased armament stockpiling, because "Germany was . . . rearming openly on a large scale, despite provisions of Part V of the Treaty of Versailles." Eight days later, on

March 12, France followed Britain's lead and doubled the period of army service and lowered the enlistment age. Hitler used these actions to justify his own military expansion. The prelude to World War II, an arms race, had begun.

Two weeks later, on March 15, Hermann Göring told the London *Daily Mail* that Germany was building up a military air force—the *Luftwaffe*. The next day, Germany reintroduced military conscription.

On May 21, Hitler secretly issued the Reich Defense Law, which placed Hjalmar Schacht in charge of economic preparations for war and reorganized the armed forces: the Reichswehr officially became the *Wehrmacht* (Armed Forces), with Hitler as its supreme commander. Defense Minister Blomberg's title was changed to minister of war. Continuing his double game that very evening in a carefully prepared speech to the Reichstag, Hitler spoke about the folly of war and declared his commitment to peace.

While Germany planned for war, Hitler turned his attention to his second obsession—his own war against the Jews of Europe. In mid-September, he attended Party Day in Nuremberg, where Germany displayed the results of its ongoing rearmament for the first time, including new tanks, armored cars, and modern aircraft. This year, the Reichstag sat in a special session at the rally, ostensibly to enact the Flag Law, an ordinance acclaiming the swastika banner as the new Reich flag. Hitler, however, used the occasion to enact two additional laws during the

SA officers take a Jewish man into custody in Berlin, 1934. (Library of Congress)

session: the State Citizenship Law and the Law for the Protection of German Blood and German Honor.

The first law declared German Jews to be subjects, not citizens, of the German state. The second law defined who was a Jew, who was an Aryan (Nordic), and who was a *Mischling* (part Jew). It also forbade marriages between Germans and Jews, and prohibited Jews from employing German servants. These laws, Hitler asserted, "repay the debt of gratitude to the movement under whose symbol [the swastika] Germany has recovered her freedom." All 250 or more subsequent anti-Semitic laws passed in Nazi Germany and throughout Europe during the next decade grew out of these citizenship and blood laws, which became known as the Nuremberg Laws.

By mid-January 1936, Hitler felt ready to embark on a dangerous campaign to acquire additional living space, which was inextricably intertwined with his hatred for the Jews. He claimed that Germany was overpopulated and lacked the natural resources to sustain its people properly. In his view, two things were needed to relieve the overcrowding and shortage of resources: more land and fewer people. These needs justified a war of expansion and a reduction of the Jewish element of the German population.

On March 7, 1936, in an operation code-named Winter Exercise, Hitler ordered a German force of nineteen infantry battalions, with artillery support, to reoccupy the Rhineland. The Rhineland comprised all German territory west of the Rhine and a thirty-mile strip east of the river, including the cities of Cologne, Düsseldorf, and Bonn, all of which the Treaty of Versailles had demilitarized and had, until 1930, been occupied by the Allies. As grounds for his aggression, Hitler cited the Franco-Soviet Pact, which France and the Soviet Union had formed as a common defense against Germany and which Hitler said threatened Germany from both the east and the west. The Wehrmacht troops crossed the Rhine with orders to withdraw at the first sign of French resistance, but there was none. While German soldiers reoccupied the Rhineland, Hitler addressed the Reichstag in Berlin. "At this moment," he said, "German troops are marching." Pandemonium erupted in his audience.

Hitler said later that a French retaliation would have

German troops cross a bridge into the Rhineland on March 7, 1936. (National Archives)

forced the Germans "to withdraw with our tails between our legs, for the military resources at our disposal would have been wholly inadequate for even a moderate resistance." The failure of either Britain or France to meet force with force enabled Hitler to seize the Rhineland without firing a shot, which emboldened him.

When a civil war erupted in Spain on July 18, 1936, Hitler provided military aid for General Francisco Franco and his nationalist forces. Hitler sent elements of his emerging Luftwaffe—known as the Condor Legion—to gain valuable military experience. The Spanish Civil War became the training ground for a greater war to come.

During the summer, Hitler drafted a Four-Year Plan for national self-sufficiency meant to put Germany's economy on a war footing. Continuing his duplicity, he served as the host of the 1936 Olympic Games held in Berlin in August. There, against a background of imperious swastika flags and banners, he proclaimed, "We are, and always will be, at peace with the world." Days later, at the Party Rally in Nuremberg in September, he announced his Four-Year Plan, declaring, "The right of the German people to live is surely as great as any other people." Hitler placed Göring in charge of Germany's economic development, a position for which he possessed little expertise.

As further indications of where Hitler's leadership was taking his nation, Germany entered into a pair of secret agreements, one with Italy on October 25 and

Hitler, accompanied by other members of the Nazi leadership, gives the Nazi salute at the opening ceremonies of the 1936 Olympic Games in Berlin. (Library of Congress)

another with Japan on November 23. Germany's new relationship with Italy covered a wide range of cooperation. A few days later, in a speech at Milan, Mussolini referred to the accord with a term that would immortalize its inherent evil: "[T]his Berlin-Rome line is not a diaphragm but rather an *axis*, around which can revolve all those European states with a will to collaboration and peace." A month later, Germany and Japan signed an anti-Soviet pact, in which they agreed to exchange information on the activities of Soviet-backed international Communist parties. Italy would join the pact the next November, and the three nations became known as the Axis Powers.

On January 30, 1937, Hitler capped his fourth year in office with a long address to the Reichstag. In his speech, he formally retracted Germany's acquiescence to those passages of the Treaty of Versailles that charged it with responsibility for World War I. "Today," he added, "I must humbly thank Providence, whose grace has enabled me, once an unknown soldier in the war, to bring to a successful issue the struggle for our honor and rights as a nation."

In four years, Hitler and the Nazis had lifted Germany out of its economic doldrums at home and raised German prestige around the world. Lavish government expenditures on public works and the improvement of the nation's resources had put people back to work and restored national confidence. He took steps to ensure a loyal corps of future followers by elevating the Nazi

The führer stands and talks with an admiring group of Hitler Youth members.
(Library of Congress)

youth movement to an agency of the state—the Hitler Youth for boys and the League of German Girls.

Hitler could now claim millions of admirers in Europe, most of whom believed the Nazi movement to be a force for good. "He did not only spread fear or aversion," recalled André François-Poncet, the French ambassador. "He excited curiosity; he awakened sympathy; his prestige grew; the force of attraction emanating from him had an impact beyond the borders of his country."

But the record shows that Hitler and the Nazis were driven from the start by one thing: power. Whatever good came out of Hitler's regime came as a by-product of his efforts to forge Germany into an instrument for achieving his goal of unbounded expansion.

Hitler continued to prepare for war. On November 5, 1937, he summoned his high command—his foreign minister; the commanders in chief of the army, navy, and air force; and his military adjutant, Colonel Friedrich Hossbach—to a secret meeting in the Reich Chancellery. At what later became known as the Hossbach Conference (because Hossbach wrote the minutes of the meeting), Hitler clarified his true intentions: "If the Führer was still living, it was his unalterable resolve to solve Germany's problem of space at the latest by 1943–45."

The fulfillment of Hitler's resolve would mean war, and two members of the high command opposed his aggressive designs—Field Marshal Werner von Blomberg, minister of war and commander in chief of the Wehrmacht, and Colonel General Freiherr Werner von Fritsch. To remove these popular and prestigious foes of his grand design, it was necessary to create a series of subterfuges and intrigues that implicated them in separate scandals. Hitler then dismissed them and thus eliminated all opposition to his planned aggressions.

In February 1938, Hitler restructured the *Oberkommando der Wehrmacht* (High Command of the Armed Forces), or OKW, appointing himself as supreme commander of the OKW and minister of war, the offices previously held by Blomberg. He replaced Fritsch with General Field Marshal Walther von Brauchitsch, and everything moved into place for his most adventurous undertaking to date—the annexation of Austria. To that purpose, Hitler invited Austrian chancellor Kurt von Schuschnigg to Berchtesgaden for a visit and forced him to sign an agreement to include members of the Austrian Nazi Party in his government. When Schuschnigg returned to Austria, however, believing that the Austrian people would reject a union with Germany, he announced a plebiscite on the issue and scheduled it for March 13. Hitler was outraged at what he considered to be Schuschnigg's duplicity and made immediate preparations to invade Austria.

Hitler had another problem to get out of the way before annexing Austria. Italy and Austria had territorial disputes stretching back centuries. The Treaty of Versailles had granted Italy the hotly disputed South Tyrol region, which had a large German population. Hitler had managed to finesse this issue, although freeing all "captive" Germans was an unwavering goal of Nazism. Now was not the time to settle this potential conflict with his Italian ally. On March 10, he sent Prince Philip of Hesse to Rome with a handwritten letter for Mussolini. His letter spoke of an Austrian conspiracy against the Reich, the suppression of a German majority in Austria, and the potential for a civil war. As a "son of the Austrian soil," he could no longer stand idly by. He must move to restore law and order to his homeland. "You, too, Your Excellency," he ventured, "could not act differently if the fate of Italy were at stake." Shortly after midnight, Hitler issued Directive

No. 1 for Operation Otto, which said, in part:

> If other measures do not succeed, I intend to march
> into Austria with armed forces in order to restore
> constitutional conditions there and to prevent further
> outrages against the nationalistic German population.
> I personally shall command the entire operation.

On March 11, at about 10:45 PM, Prince Philip tele-phoned Hitler from Rome with the impatiently awaited response from the Italian dictator: "The Duce accepted the whole affair in a very, very friendly manner. He sends you his cordial regards."

Hitler replied, "Then please tell Mussolini I shall never forget him for this."

The next afternoon, bells pealed in Austria as Hitler crossed the border at his birthplace of Braunau, and thousands of people lined the streets of flower-decked villages along the four-hour route to Linz. From the balcony of the town hall in Linz, he delivered a short speech with conspicuous emotion:

> If Providence once called me from this city to assume
> the leadership of the Reich, it must have charged me
> with a mission, and that mission can only have been
> to restore my dear homeland to the German Reich.

Hitler's enthusiastic reception by the people of Aus-tria persuaded him to annex Austria outright the next day, March 13. In a Hitler-driven plebiscite in April,

Austrians and Germans approved the *Anschluss* (union) and the Nazi Party by a 99 percent majority vote. Once again Hitler had contravened the terms of a World War I settlement—this time, the Treaty of St. Germain—and had kicked sand in the face of the Allies. England and France protested the German annexation, but once again they chose not to contest Hitler's actions.

Hitler turned his focus next to the Sudetenland. The ease Hitler experienced in annexing Austria encouraged him to use a similar approach in the mountainous land between Bohemia and Silesia. The Treaty of St. Germain had awarded the Sudetenland to the new state of Czecho-slovakia in 1919. Hitler directed his ally Konrad Henlein, the Sudeten German Party leader, to agitate for impossible demands on behalf of the region's 3.25 million German-speaking residents. Hitler planned to use the pretext of the maltreatment of Germans as an excuse to march into the Sudetenland and claim it for the Third Reich.

On May 30, 1938, Hitler called his top generals together for a conference at the artillery school at Jüterbog, about sixty miles south of Berlin, and told them, "It is my unalterable will to smash Czechoslovakia by military action in the near future." He set October 1 as the date to commence Operation Green.

On September 12, at the closing ceremony of the last party rally in Nuremberg, Hitler spoke to more than a million people. He condemned the Czechs for supposed mistreatment of the Sudeten Germans. "The Germans in

Czechoslovakia are neither defenseless nor are they deserted," he warned, "and people should take notice of that fact." He paused to the thunderous roar of "Sieg Heil! Sieg Heil!" from the audience. Then, in a conciliatory tone, he added, "We should be sorry if this were to disturb or damage our relations with other European nations, but the blame does not lie with us!" The ensuing crisis dwarfed the earlier events in Austria—Europe appeared headed for war.

At the height of tension, Hitler acceded to Mussolini's suggestion to call for a four-party conference, consisting of Germany, Great Britain, France, and Italy, to resolve the Sudeten crisis. The meeting was scheduled for September 29. Three days before the conference, Hitler addressed a mass meeting at Berlin's Sports Palace and assured British prime minister Neville Chamberlain and the rest of the world that he intended to make no further territorial claims beyond the Sudetenland:

> We have come now to the last problem which has to be solved. It is the last territorial demand that I have to make in Europe. In 1919, 3,500,000 Germans were torn away from their compatriots by a company of mad statesmen. The Czech State originated in a huge lie and the name of the liar is Beneš [Czech statesman and president, Eduard Beneš].

Chamberlain, convinced that his nation was unprepared for war, made a third trip to Germany to plead for peace. "I should still say it was right to attempt it," he rationalized afterward. "The only alternative is war." Chamberlain, together with French premier Édouard Daladier, who also felt that his nation was not ready for war, persuaded the Czechs to accept Hitler's territorial demands and signed the Munich Agreement on September 30, 1938. Chamberlain flew back to Britain and announced, "I believe it is peace for our time."

The Munich Agreement left Czechoslovakia defenseless. The Wehrmacht occupied the Sudetenland during the first ten days of October 1938 and incorpo-

The 1938 Munich Agreement, while giving the world a momentary hope for peace, doomed Czechoslovakia and encouraged Hitler's land-grabbing. From left to right, the signers of the agreement: Neville Chamberlain, Édouard Daladier, Hitler, Benito Mussolini, and Italian foreign minister Galeazzo Ciano. (The National Archives)

rated it into Germany. Poland took advantage of the situation to seize the small industrial and mining border district of Teschen, which was populated by a Polish minority. In the east, most of Slovakia, which was controlled by the Slovak People's Party, opted to become a vassal state of Germany, while Hungary grabbed pieces of southern Slovakia and Ruthenia. All that remained of Czechoslovakia was Bohemia and Moravia, both of which Hitler occupied on March 15, 1939. Eight days later, Hitler demanded the return of Memel, Germany's former Baltic seaport, from Lithuania. Lithuania complied immediately.

After each expansion of Germany's borders, Hitler assured Europe and the world that he had no further territorial aspirations. Europe and the world might have done well to question Hitler's sincerity when he and Mussolini signed an agreement on May 22, 1939, in which Germany and Italy agreed to "act side by side and with united forces to secure their living space." The treaty, known as the Pact of Steel, also pledged that each nation would act "immediately" to aid the other militarily if either "became involved in warlike complications."

Hitler's next diplomatic move stunned the world. The core ideology of Nazism was an attack on communism and the Russian Bolsheviks who had seized power in 1917. In speeches, Hitler had linked the imagined vast Jewish conspiracy with communism. But in August 1939, he and Joseph Stalin, dictator of the Communist Soviet

WONDER HOW LONG THE HONEYMOON WILL LAST?

This American cartoon remarks on the surprising alliance between Hitler and Joseph Stalin. (Library of Congress)

Union, signed a nonaggression pact. Observers could only wonder what the alliance of two bitter enemies could mean to Europe and the world.

Eight

HITLER'S WARS

Poland's vast expanse made it the next victim of Lebensraum. But first, Hitler needed a pretense to plunge Europe into another war. He signed Directive No. 1 for the Conduct of the War. It said, in part:

> In the West it is essential to let the responsibility for initiating hostilities be placed unequivocally upon England and France. . . . The neutrality of Holland, Belgium, Luxemburg and Switzerland, which we have guaranteed, is to be scrupulously observed.

The scenario centered on a small German radio station in Gleiwitz (Gliwice), just inside Germany on the Polish frontier. At noon on August 31, 1939, Nazi soldiers drugged and shot approximately one dozen prisoners from a nearby concentration camp. That night, at about eight o'clock, SS Major Alfred Naujocks led a band of SS men dressed in Polish uniforms in a mock attack on the radio station in Gleiwitz. They fired a few pistol shots and quickly departed, leaving behind the corpses of the previously murdered concentration camp inmates. Provocation for a German attack on Poland had thereby been established.

An hour later, all German radio stations broadcast a sixteen-point list of German demands. Hitler had never submitted his proposals to Poland, making it impossible for them to be complied with.

At 4:45 AM on September 1, the precise time designated by Directive No. 1, the German cruiser *Schleswig-Holstein*, which was then in Danzig (present day Gdansk) harbor on a courtesy visit, opened fire on a Polish fortress. Simultaneously, German armies surged across the German-Polish border to "avenge" the Polish aggression on the radio station. World War II had begun.

That morning at ten o'clock, Hitler delivered a speech to the Reichstag in which he condemned "the numerous Polish attacks on German territory, among them an attack by regular Polish troops on the Gleiwitz transmitter." Continuing, he pledged once more to dedicate his life to the service of Germany:

> I am asking of no German more than I myself was ready to perform during the four years of World War I. The German people will suffer no hardships which I do not suffer. My whole life henceforth belongs more

than ever to my people. I am from now on nothing
more than the first soldier of the Reich. I have once
more put on the [uniform] coat that was most sacred
and dear to me. I will not take it off again until victory
is assured, or I will not survive the outcome.

Despite British and French guarantees of Polish independence asserted earlier in the year, Hitler believed
that Great Britain and France would remain neutral.
They had not stood by Czechoslovakia the year before.
This time, however, Britain and France honored their
commitment to Poland and declared war on Germany on
September 3.

In great sweeping thrusts, German tanks and mecha-
nized infantry, supported by dive-bombers, introduced
a new kind of warfare to Poland and the world in the first
days of September 1939—the *Blitzkrieg* (lightning war).
Within three days, the Luftwaffe had destroyed most of
the Polish air force and controlled the skies. Stalin,
protected from invasion by his pact with Hitler and eager
to grab a slice of Poland, ordered his troops to attack on
September 17, and soon the Soviet Union claimed the
eastern half of Poland. With nothing but horse cavalry
and riflemen, the Polish army fought bravely against
tanks and armored divisions and managed to hold them
off for four weeks before collapsing in the face of the
devastating Nazi onslaught. On September 27, the Polish government fled to Romania.

The Soviets carved out a bigger slice of the territorial
pie in Eastern Europe than suited Hitler, including the

In a desperate and poignant move, the outdated Polish cavalry attempted to take on the powerful Panzer tanks and armored divisions of the German forces to protect their homeland.

Borislav-Drohobycz oil region, but he postponed taking any action against his new allies. That could come later. Hitler had hoped that Great Britain and France would want to negotiate a peace. When they did not, he moved ahead with preparations for a second blitzkrieg in the West. He also began to plan for an invasion of the Soviet Union.

On November 23, 1939, Hitler summoned his commanding generals and general staff officers and told them of his decision to attack the West. "My decision is unchangeable," he said. Because of the harsh winter weather conditions, Hitler's commanders persuaded him to wait until spring to attack, and the war settled into a six-month lull that became known to the British as the Phony War and to the Germans as the *Sitzkrieg* (Sit-down War).

Meanwhile, Hitler pressed forward with his persecution of the Jews and other groups he considered undesirable, including Slavs and Roma (commonly called Gypsies). On August 18, 1939, he established the Reich Committee for the Scientific Registration of Serious Hereditary and Congenitally Based Diseases, with headquarters at Tiergartenstrasse 4 in Berlin. Registration of malformed children began in August, followed by the registration of asylum inmates (mentally challenged men, women, and children) in September. A euthanasia program known as *Aktion T4* (Operation T4; the "T4" was derived from the address of its headquarters) began in October. The first large-scale killings with carbon monoxide gas, mainly of malformed children and the mentally handicapped, took place in Pomerania and East Prussia. Between October 1939 and August 1941, when the program was terminated, Aktion T4 euthanized about 100,000 "lives not worth living" (as Hitler termed them).

In September, Jews in Germany were forbidden to own radios and were subjected to an 8:00 PM curfew. SD chief Reinhard Heydrich issued orders for the establishment of ghettos in Nazi-occupied Poland. On October 6, Hitler, speaking to the Reichstag, outlined a plan for isolating Jews from the rest of German society. He wanted to begin the process of transporting Jews and other groups to concentration camps or to fixed locations to be used as forced labor. The next day, Hitler appointed Heinrich Himmler Reich commissioner for the Consolidation of German Nationhood to oversee the resettlement program.

Five days later, on October 12, Hitler named his

In Warsaw, residents board a streetcar designated specifically for Jews. Polish Jews were forced to register with the authorities and were confined to the ghetto. Their forced removal to concentration camps began in the fall of 1939.
(Library of Congress)

lawyer, Hans Frank, the chief civilian officer and governor general for occupied Poland. Frank described his policy: "Poland shall be treated like a colony: the Poles will become the slaves of the Greater German Empire." The eastward evacuation of Jews from Vienna began that same day. Millions more would follow, driven from Germany and German-occupied nations across Europe.

With the coming of spring 1940, Hitler shifted his focus to the western front. In mid-March, he met briefly with Mussolini to discuss Italy's entry into the war. The Italian dictator agreed to join in but at a time of his own choosing, "when the Allies were so shaken by the German attack that it needed only a second blow to bring them to their knees."

Hitler moved first into Denmark and Norway on April 9 to preempt any British attempt to establish operating bases in the two Scandinavian countries. On May 10, his armies smashed simultaneously into Holland, Belgium, Luxembourg, and France. That same day, in London, Neville Chamberlain resigned as Britain's prime minister and Winston Churchill moved into No. 10 Downing Street, the prime minister's official residence.

The Wehrmacht drove through the Low Countries and deep into France with lightning speed, reaching the English Channel ports—a goal the Germans had failed to reach in World War I—in just ten days. Holland fell after five days; Belgium surrendered ten days later. Hitler, taking a personal hand in the drive across France, halted General Karl von Rundstedt's tanks a few miles south of the French port of Dunkirk on May 24. He wanted to preserve his armor for the drive on Paris, which would decide France's fate. His interference frustrated the German plan to encircle the British Expeditionary Force (BEF) before it escaped across the Channel. The British and French were able to evacuate an estimated 338,226 troops between May 26 and June 3. For the most part, however, the German blitzkrieg across western Europe was a huge success, capped by Italy's entry into the war as Germany's ally on June 10, the occupation of Paris on June 14, and the fall of France on June 21.

Three days earlier, on June 18, Prime Minister Winston Churchill, who had already been informed of

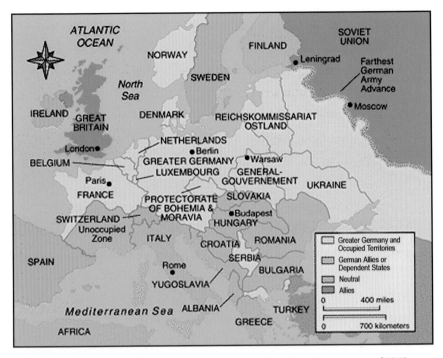

This map shows the extent of Hitler's empire at its peak in the summer of 1942.

France's imminent collapse, addressed the House of Commons. He declared Great Britain's determination to fight on, irrespective of the odds, "so that, if the British Empire and its Commonwealth last for a thousand years, men will still say: 'This was their finest hour.'"

On June 22, Hitler accepted the French surrender in the forest of Compiègne in the same place and in the same railway car in which the German delegation had signed the armistice agreement with the Allies on November 11, 1918. Hitler savored the moment with a tour of Paris the next day. Stopping at the Hôtel des Invalides, founded by Louis XIV to quarter 7,000 aged or invalid veterans, he stared down at the tomb of Napoleon and murmured, "This is the greatest and finest moment of my life." Berliners welcomed him home at the start of July with cheers, torrents of flowers, and the pealing of bells.

Hitler hoped France's surrender would persuade Great Britain to seek a negotiated peace. When the British held fast to Churchill's stated resolve to fight on, Hitler issued Directive No. 16 on the Preparation of a Landing Operation against England, which began: "Since England, despite her militarily hopeless situation, still shows no sign of willingness to come to terms, I have decided to prepare a landing operation against England, and if necessary to carry it out." The invasion plan was code-named Operation Sea Lion.

Newly promoted Reich marshal Hermann Göring boasted to the German high command that the destruction of the Fighter Command of the Royal Air Force (RAF) would take four days; elimination of the rest of the RAF would take a little longer, from two to four weeks. But the Luftwaffe, which had failed to destroy RAF air cover over Dunkirk, also failed to come through during the ensuing Battle of Britain. The RAF fighters managed to hold off Göring's numerically superior Luftwaffe in the summer and autumn of 1940. This failure to control the skies over Great Britain forced Hitler to postpone Operation Sea Lion on September 17 and to abandon it on October 12.

Meanwhile, on August 15, while planes and pilots battled over Great Britain, Adolf Eichmann formally submitted a carefully prepared, fourteen-page memorandum on the "Jewish question." Eichmann, an SD officer who specialized in Jewish affairs, advocated the deportation of Jews en masse to Madagascar, the world's fourth-largest island (226,657 square miles), located about 250 miles off the southeast coast of Africa. The Nazis entertained the idea for several months but eventually dropped it in favor of a more permanent solution. In the meantime, the deportations of Jews to concentration camps continued.

Although the Battle of Britain continued unsuccessfully—and Hitler grew increasingly outraged at Göring's

✠ CONCENTRATION CAMPS

Prisoners lie in their bunks at Buchenwald concentration camp. (National Archives)

The Nazis established more than forty concentration camps, some of which had multiple sub-camps, in eastern Europe, mainly in Germany and Poland. Some were collection points where prisoners were held before being shipped out to more permanent facilities. Others were labor camps where prisoners were forced to work to fuel Germany's war machine. And some, the most infamous, were extermination camps.

More than a million people died at Auschwitz-Birkenau, and a similar number at Treblinka, both camps in Poland. Buchenwald, in Germany, was technically a labor camp but conditions were so poor that tens of thousands died there—some from the cold, malnutrition, starvation, or disease, while others were victims of medical experiments or mass exterminations. Bergen-Belsen, the German camp where Anne Frank and her sister Margot died, was initially a prisoner-of-war camp and then became a concentration camp for political prisoners. At least 50,000 died there.

The following list of extermination camps gives their location and the minimum number of people killed in each. Exact figures will never be known.

Auschwitz-Birkenau (Poland)	1,100,000
Belzec (Poland)	600,000
Chelmno (Poland)	340,000
Majdanek (Poland)	235,000
Maly Trostenets (Belarus)	200,000-500,000
Sobibór (Poland)	250,000
Treblinka (Poland)	800,000
Warsaw (Poland)	200,000

failure against the RAF—Hitler turned his attention back to the east and the south. Hitler had always considered his pact with Stalin to be temporary. On December 18, 1940, he made his intentions toward Russia clear to his military comrades. Directive No. 21 began "The German Wehrmacht must be prepared *to crush Soviet Russia in a quick campaign* even before the conclusion of the war against England."

Stalin had taken advantage of their 1939 pact, and Hitler's occupation with France and Great Britain, to occupy the Baltic states of Lithuania, Latvia, and Estonia. Stalin also demanded two provinces in Romania, which aroused the territorial ambitions of Romania's neighbors, Hungary and Bulgaria.

Romania was critically important because of its valuable oil fields. Germany's armies, with their blitzkrieg attacks, were heavily dependent on oil, which had to come from outside. Romania had some of Europe's richest oil fields.

Another area rich in oil was North Africa. That was yet another reason to commit troops to North African and Balkan campaigns. Mussolini rashly invaded Greece in the fall of 1940 and soon ran into difficulty. At the same time, Italian forces in North Africa were proving to be no match for British troops fighting desperately to hold onto British colonial possessions in the region.

These two forces—the need for oil and the necessity of propping up Mussolini—forced Hitler to postpone the invasion of the Soviet Union planned to begin in early spring of 1941. First he had to stabilize the situation in the Balkans, including Greece, and North Africa. Hitler's intervention in the Mediterranean theater delayed the Soviet invasion, code-named Operation Barbarossa, for about five weeks. Meanwhile, German troops continued to mass along the Soviet border.

Finally, Yugoslavia and Greece were occupied and the tide was temporarily turned in Germany's favor in North Africa. General Erwin Rommel's Afrika Korps moved toward Egypt. The famous Russian winter, which had done so much to destroy Napoleon's army in 1812, had always loomed over Operation Barbarossa. Hitler could wait no longer. On June 22, 1941, at 3:30 AM, three German army groups, comprising 153 divisions—reinforced by

35.5 satellite divisions and supported by 2,740 aircraft—smashed across the Soviet border in a line stretching intermittently from the Baltic Sea to the Black Sea. On the eve of the invasion, Hitler revealed his feelings about the coming campaign in a letter to Mussolini:

> Since I struggled through to this decision, I again feel spiritually free. The partnership with the Soviet Union, in spite of the complete sincerity of my efforts to bring about a final conciliation, was nevertheless often very irksome to me, for in some way or other it seemed to me to be a break with my whole origin, my concepts and my former obligations. I am happy now to be delivered from this torment.

The attack apparently caught Stalin by surprise, but he quickly recovered his footing. The Soviets and the British signed a mutual assistance pact in Moscow on July 12, ending any hope that the arch anti-Communist Churchill would form an alliance with Germany against the Soviets. On July 28, Hitler moved into the *Wolfsschanze* (wolf's lair)—his field headquarters at Rastenburg, East Prussia. He would remain there until March 20, 1943, often making key military decisions that scattered—rather than concentrated—his forces and eventually led to the dilution of the German attack.

Hitler was convinced the collapse of the Soviet Union would come in about six weeks. In the beginning, his optimism seemed to be well founded. German armies advanced two-thirds of the way to Moscow in only twenty-six days. Hitler then, against the advice of his generals, made a serious blunder when he diverted part of his forces to achieve a crushing victory over the Soviets at Kiev. This diversion, along with the five-week delay in launching Barbarossa, proved decisive. Soon autumn rains had turned the roads to mud and the German advance on Moscow slowed to a crawl. Nevertheless, by November 5, the Germans had almost encircled Moscow. The Soviets managed to turn away a German thrust on the city. Then the harsh Russian winter set in early. Soon snow rendered the roads impassable. Arctic cold caused machines to malfunction and the soldiers to freeze to death in their summer clothing.

In December, Hitler called off further offensive operations until the following spring. Then the Soviets

This stylized color photograph shows German troops on the outskirts of Moscow in January 1942. (Courtesy of the Granger Collection.)

surprised him and his commanders by launching a savage attack on December 6, 1941. Unlike the German soldiers, whom Hitler had forbidden from packing winter clothes as an incentive to make them move faster, the Soviet troops were properly clothed. The Soviet attack, under the command of General Zhukov, forced the Germans backward about forty miles. In January 1942, the Germans began a bitter, three-and-a-half year retreat that would end with the Soviet occupation of Berlin.

On December 7, 1941, Japan, Hitler's Axis partner, attacked the United States naval base at Pearl Harbor, Hawaii, as well as other U.S. and British military installations in the Far East. Hitler, true to his tripartite commitment—however ill advised—declared war on the United States on December 11. Italy did the same. Hitler believed that Japan would keep the Americans occupied until he had time to defeat the Soviets. At the end of 1941, Hitler dismissed army commander in chief Walter von Brauchitsch and assumed field command himself.

While Hitler's Wehrmacht advanced first across Poland and later across the vast Soviet countryside, SS special action groups known as *Einsatzgruppen* (task forces) followed the advancing armies to wage a different kind of war. First organized by Heinrich Himmler and his underling Reinhard Heydrich in 1939, the Einsatzgruppen were initially assigned the task of murdering national leaders and rounding up Jews for confinement in ghettos. At the outset of Operation Barbarossa, they had again followed the armies but their orders now called for the extermination of all Jews and all Soviet government officials. Hitler put nothing in writing regarding his policy toward the extermination of the Jews but did issue the Commissar Decree on June 6, 1941, prior to the invasion of the Soviet Union. His decree stated, in part:

> The war against Russia cannot be fought in a knightly fashion. The struggle is one of ideologies and racial differences and will have to be waged with unprecedented, unmerciful, and unrelenting hardness. . . . Any German soldier who breaks international law will be pardoned. Russia did not take part in the Hague Convention and, therefore, has no rights under it.

Under the pretext of military necessity, the Einsatzgruppen set about their tasks initially by mass shootings but soon realized a more efficient, less expensive means of mass killing was needed. On July 31, 1941, Hermann Göring ordered Reinhard Heydrich, now chief of the Reich Security Central Office (RSHA), the main security department of the Nazi government, to submit a comprehensive plan for "a final solution of the Jewish question."

Nine

BRINGING DOWN THE WORLD

At 11:00 AM on January 20, 1942, fifteen men gathered in a conference room at Reich Security Central Office headquarters in Grossen-Wannsee. The men represented various agencies of the Nazi government, including the East Ministry, the Office of the Four-Year Plan, the Ministry of Justice, the General Government of Poland, and the Foreign Ministry. RSHA chief Heinrich Heydrich chaired the meeting and told those assembled that he had been charged with "the responsibility for working out the final solution of the Jewish problem regardless of geographical boundaries." Adolf Eichmann, head of the new Race and Resettlement Office, recorded the minutes of the meeting.

Heydrich presented the broad outline of his plan. It

Heinrich Heydrich.

Adolf Eichmann.

called for the evacuation of all Jews to the east, where they would be organized into huge labor columns in which most would "fall through natural diminution." Those who survived the hard labor were to be "treated accordingly," that is, exterminated, to keep them from establishing a "germ cell of a new Jewish development."

The Wannsee Conference, as it is known, ended about four in the afternoon. After the meeting, Heydrich, Eichmann, and Gestapo chief Heinrich Müller gathered "cozily around a fireplace," drinking and singing songs. "After a while," Eichmann recalled, "we climbed onto the chairs and drank a toast; then onto the table and traipsed round and round—on the chairs and on the table again." Some of the attendees believed that Hitler was not fully aware of the mass murder being plotted at

Wannsee, but this trio knew better. They saw themselves as instruments of the führer and thus free of any personal guilt. "Who was I to judge?" Eichmann testified later. "Who was I to have my own thoughts in this matter?"

In the presence of Himmler a few days later, Hitler commented that if the Jews "refuse to go voluntarily I see no other solution but extermination." In a subsequent speech at the Sports Palace, he said, "We realize that this war can only end either in the wiping out of the Germanic nations, or by the disappearance of Jewry from Europe." Although no direct, written evidence of Hitler's culpability in the Final Solution has been uncovered, there can be no doubt that the absolute leader of the Third Reich, the man who could divide and divert whole armies on the eastern front, was involved in the genocide. He left the details to Himmler, Heydrich, Eichmann, and a host of other willing executioners, but the Final Solution was the culmination of Hitler's decades-old dream.

With the dismissal of Army Commander in Chief Brauchitsch, Hitler became not only supreme commander of the German armed forces but also *Feldherr*, leader of the armies in the field. During the next nine months, the German armies continued to make advancements, both in northern Africa on the frontier of Egypt and in the lower reaches of the Caucasus Mountains in Russia. These achievements were due more to the army's fighting professionalism than to any strategic or tactical insight on Hitler's part.

Hitler's battlefront leadership was merciless and uncompromising, sometimes insightful but usually flawed. Field Marshal Erich von Manstein, commander of Army Group Don and later Army Group South on the Eastern Front, provided a keen appraisal of his führer as aspiring warlord:

> He was a man who saw fighting only in terms of the utmost brutality. His way of thinking conformed more to a mental picture of masses of the enemy bleeding to death before our lines than to the conception of a subtle fencer who knows how to make an occasional step backwards in order to lunge for the decisive thrust. For the art of war he substituted a brutal force which, as he saw it, was guaranteed maximum effectiveness by the will-power behind.

When the fighting resumed in the spring of 1942, Hitler—again contrary to the counsel of his best military advisors—insisted on shifting the main focus of the German attack in the Soviet Union to the south. He wanted to seize the oil fields. For a time, the German armies advanced rapidly into the Crimea and beyond during the summer of 1942.

General Friedrich von Paulus's German Sixth Army commenced an assault on Stalingrad on August 19, 1942. After two months of savage fighting in the ruins of the city, the Soviets launched a counterattack with over a million men, gradually isolating and decimating most of the German Sixth Army. Although, as the bitter

This captured painting from the Russian front, entitled "German Soldiers Entrenched," provides a sharp contrast from the self-assured appearance of earlier days in the Nazi regime. (Captured German painting, U.S. Army)

Russian winter set in, it was obvious the attack on Stalingrad had failed, Hitler refused to concede defeat. As late as January 25, 1943 he ordered:

> Surrender is forbidden. Sixth Army will hold their position to the last man and last round, and by their heroic endurance will make an unforgettable contribution toward the establishment of a defensive front and the salvation of the Western World.

On January 30, 1943, when Hitler elevated Paulus to field marshal, he reminded him that no German field marshal had ever surrendered. But this time even Hitler's wishes went unheeded. Paulus surrendered what remained of the German Sixth Army the next day. The destruction of the Sixth Army at Stalingrad led to the abandonment of Hitler's Caucasus campaign. Afterward, Hitler spoke of Paulus with contempt for not committing suicide.

The tide was turning in North Africa as well. On November 4, 1942, Lieutenant General Bernard L. Montgomery's British Eighth Army defeated Field Marshal Erwin Rommel's *Panzerarmee* (Panzer Army) in the second battle of Alamein, about sixty-five miles west of Alexandria, Egypt. Rommel had no choice but to flee headlong to the west. Four days later, on November 8, an Anglo-American invasion force, commanded by American lieutenant general Dwight D. Eisenhower, landed in Morocco and Algeria. Eisenhower's forces advanced toward the east while Montgomery's army drove to the west, trapping Rommel between them.

Despite repeated pleas from Rommel to evacuate the Axis forces from North Africa and save them to fight another day elsewhere, Hitler clung tenaciously to his policy of no retreat. The final reckoning for the Axis forces in North Africa came on May 6, 1943. "The front collapsed," Rommel later wrote. "[T]here were no more arms and no ammunition and it was all over. The Army surrendered." Hitler's refusal to evacuate the Axis army caused him to lose 250,000 troops to the Allies, along with untold tons of supplies.

For the next two years, Hitler presided over the retreat of his armies on all fronts—in Sicily and Italy, all along the eastern front, and finally—after the Normandy landings on June 6, 1944—on the western front. On July 25, 1943, with the Allies already controlling Sicily and preparing to invade the Italian peninsula, Mussolini was deposed, ending his Fascist regime. Later he and his mistress were murdered by Italian partisans fighting with the Allies. Despite Italy's capitulation, Hitler refused to allow his German troops to escape the Italian peninsula.

The defeats on the battlefield were aggravated by increasingly intense Allied bombings of German cities and military-industrial installations. American day bombers joined with British night bombers in around-the-clock bombing raids. At sea, German U-boats were lost faster than they could be replaced. By the end of 1943, Germany had lost the battle of the Atlantic, which limited its ability to import oil and other supplies.

The mental and physical strain of shouldering a collapsing two-front war began to show on Hitler. At age fifty-four, he began to experience a trembling of his left arm and left leg that grew steadily worse. He attempted to control it by bracing his foot against a convenient object and holding his left hand with his right. And when he walked, he started to drag his left foot as if lame. He complained of stomach pains and suspected that he had

The führer with his loyal shepherd, Blondi. Shortly before committing suicide, Hitler killed Blondi by feeding her a tablet of cyanide. (Courtesy of the Granger Collection.)

a weak heart. He had placed himself in the care of a doctor, Professor Theodor Morell, in 1936. The professor diagnosed Hitler's main malady as "intestinal exhaustion," which appealed to Hitler's hypochondriacal tendencies. Over the next nine years, Hitler submitted himself to treatments involving a wide range of prescriptions, including amphetamines, to which he might have become addicted.

Hitler's orders became more difficult to carry out after the Allied invasion of Normandy in June 1944. Commanders of his fighting forces in France found it increasingly difficult to receive clear orders from a supreme commander who was headquartered far to the east, in Wolfsschanze or Berlin, and preoccupied with the eastern front. No matter how skillfully or valiantly his troops performed, they were undermined by a führer who was too distant, too fanatically stubborn to authorize strategic withdrawals, and too overburdened with responsibilities to make sound decisions in a timely manner.

On July 2, 1944, Field Marshal Karl von Rundstedt, now commander of the German Army Group West, called Field Marshal Wilhelm Keitel, chief of the German high command, to apprise him of the deteriorating situation in Normandy and of the futility of continuing the war. A distraught Keitel asked, "What shall we do?" Rundstedt replied acidly, "Make peace, you fools. What else can you do?" Hitler replaced Rundstedt with Field Marshal Günther von Kluge the next morning.

Over the years, Hitler's antagonists made numerous unsuccessful attempts on his life. The most well-known and thoroughly documented assassination attempt occurred on July 20, 1944. By then, many German military officers wanted an end to the war, and they knew that Hitler would prolong it to the last possible moment. They saw killing Hitler as their only solution.

The most serious conspiracy to remove Hitler began to unfold when Count Claus Schenk Graf von Stauffenberg—a war hero who had lost an eye, his right arm, and two fingers of his left hand in Northern Africa—carried a preset bomb in a briefcase into a concrete briefing hut at the Wolf's Lair at 12:37 PM. He placed it behind a sturdy oak table leg, about twelve feet from Hitler, who was poring over the day's reports.

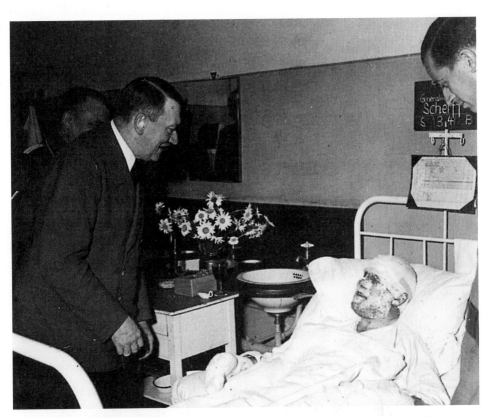

Not long after the assassination attempt, a largely unharmed Hitler visits with one of the victims of the bombing. (National Archives)

Stauffenberg left immediately after placing the bomb. The explosion went off at 12:45 PM, killing one man instantly and severely wounding several others of the twenty-four men present. Three later died of their wounds.

Hitler, who was shielded from the full blast by the oak table leg, staggered from the hut. His hair and right leg were burned, his right arm partially paralyzed, and his eardrums damaged. Convinced that Providence had spared him to complete his mission on earth, he kept repeating to Dr. Morell, "I am invulnerable, I am immortal!"

The conspirators in the July bomb plot were quickly rounded up and executed. Stauffenberg was shot at midnight in the courtyard of the War Ministry. Hitler watched home movies of the hangings of the other principal conspirators throughout the night.

Despite his stated confidence, Hitler was becoming desperate. Allied forces pressed on him from the east, the west, and the south. Allied aircraft ravaged his beloved Fatherland from above. He began to put his hope in the variety of secret weapons that were under development. He became convinced that the V-1 flying bomb, the V-2 rocket, and the Messerschmitt Me-262 jet aircraft would compel the Western Allies to end their bombing and might even drive them off the continent. After an Allied air raid on Munich, an enraged Hitler vowed vengeance to his mistress, Eva Braun, who was spending more time with him as the military situation worsened, and told her about his new rocket. "Panic will break out in England!" he said. Although the "V" weapons succeeded in terrorizing a few communities in Great Britain and Belgium in 1944 and 1945, they were highly inaccurate. None of the other weapons worked out, primarily because of Hitler's constant interference in their design and production.

The incessant Allied bombings grew more intense as the war wore on. In May 1944, Albert Speer reported the destructive effects of American daylight bombing raids on fuel plants in central and eastern Germany. "The enemy has struck us at one of our weakest points," he told Hitler. "If they persist this time, we will soon no longer have any fuel production worth mentioning."

The führer grew increasingly stubborn as the encircling Allied armies closed the ring around him. He refused to accept defeat or to entertain any notion of a negotiated peace. He still clung to the belief that Providence would miraculously intervene to make possible that glorious victory he thought was his destiny.

In mid-September 1944, Hitler summoned OKW chief Field Marshal Wilhelm Keitel and several of his senior commanders to a special conference at the Wolf's Lair. To their astonishment, Hitler announced, "I have just made a momentous decision. I shall go over to the counterattack." He jabbed a finger at a spot on a map and said, "Here, out of the Ardennes, with the objective— Antwerp!"

Hitler envisioned a sudden, swift thrust through the Allied lines in the wooded Ardennes region of eastern Belgium and Luxembourg, splitting the British and American armies and capturing the Belgian port of Antwerp. This masterful stroke would force the Allies— for reasons clear only to Hitler—to open peace negotiations. Field Marshal Karl von Rundstedt, the German commander in the west, assessed the plan in private: "If we reach the Meuse [River], we should get down on our knees and thank God." Field Marshal Walther Model, one of his field commanders, agreed.

In the early hours of December 16, 1944, Hitler launched the Ardennes offensive—more popularly known as the Battle of the Bulge. The offensive caught the Allied armies by surprise and did succeed in driving

American troops hold off the Germans in the Battle of the Bulge, the last major European conflict of World War II.

a bulge in the U.S. First Army's lines. But the Allied armies quickly stemmed the German advance and began to push them back. The Ardennes offensive—Hitler's last great gamble—ended in a crushing German defeat and the restoration of the American lines.

Hitler's gamble cost him almost 200,000 casualties, virtually destroyed the Luftwaffe and most of his reserve forces, and hastened the end of the war in Europe. His generals knew the war was lost. Hitler knew it, too, but he refused to consider surrender. In mid-January 1945, he vowed, "We'll not capitulate. Never. We can go down. But we'll take a world with us."

❧ Ten

LAST DAYS

In mid-January 1945, shortly after the Soviets had begun a new offensive in the east, Hitler returned to Berlin and reestablished his headquarters in the bombed-out Reich Chancellery. Stepped-up Allied air raids often forced Hitler and his military staff to seek shelter in the underground quarters known as the *Führerbunker* (leader bunker), fifty feet beneath the chancellery and its garden. Those who saw him at this time described him as an ashen-faced old man, with a shuffling gait and a trembling arm and leg. General Heinz Guderian, who saw him often, wrote, "It was no longer simply his left hand, but the whole left side of his body that trembled. . . . He walked awkwardly, stooped more than ever, and his gestures were jerky and slow. He had to have a chair pushed beneath him when he wished to sit down."

Like the walls of the chancellery, Hitler's Nazi regime was collapsing around him. On January 27, 1945, Soviet troops liberated the death camp at Auschwitz, and the secret horrors of the Holocaust became known to the world. Only 7,000 emaciated survivors of a Nazi extermination process that killed an estimated six million Jews were found at Auschwitz.

Three days later, on January 30, Hitler spoke on the radio to the German people for the last time. He denounced international Jewry and Asiatic Bolshevism and implored every German to do his or her duty to the last. In conclusion, he said:

> However grave the crisis may be at the moment, it will, despite everything, finally be mastered by our unalterable will, by our readiness for sacrifice and by our abilities. We shall overcome this calamity, too, and this fight, too, will not be won by central Asia but by Europe; and at its head will be the nation that has represented Europe against the East for 1500 years and shall represent it for all times: our Greater German Reich, the German nation.

In three months, beginning with the start of the Soviet offensive on January 12 and carrying through to April 12, when the U.S. Ninth Army crossed the Elbe River, the Allies scored one victory after another. On March 19, Hitler shocked even his close associates when he initiated a scorched-earth policy, ordering the destruction of all factories, supply depots, railways, bridges, water and electrical installations, and communications systems to keep them from falling into the hands of the enemy. While the orders had a military justification, Hitler's anger was directed toward the German people, whom he was convinced had failed him. In defeat, he would leave them nothing:

> If the war is to be lost, the nation will also perish. This fate is inevitable. There is no need to consider the basis of a most primitive existence any longer. On the contrary it is better to destroy even that, and to destroy it ourselves.

The Soviets entered Vienna on April 13 and crossed the Oder River, a scant forty-five miles from the führerbunker, three days later. That same day, Joseph Goebbels, now in charge of gathering all manpower for a last-ditch fight against the Allies, learned of the death of U.S. president Franklin D. Roosevelt. He telephoned the news at once to Hitler. "My Führer, I congratulate you!" he shouted excitedly. "It is written in the stars that the second half of April will be the turning point for us. Today is Friday, April 13. It is the turning point!" Three days later, on April 16, a Soviet army of 2.5 million men commenced the final assault on Berlin.

In mid-April, Eva Braun arrived in Berlin, against Hitler's orders. She insisted on sharing Hitler's fate. Despite his protests, he was clearly cheered by her

Ever devoted to Hitler, Eva Braun looks on as the führer naps. (National Archives)

appearance at the führerbunker and touched by her willingness to share his fate.

With the battle for Berlin raging in the streets outside, talk in the führerbunker now concentrated on whether the führer should remain in Berlin or flee to the Bavarian Alps to make a last stand. Goebbels's sense of mystical egotism may have influenced his final decision. If necessary, Goebbels suggested, the führer should leave the earth in a blinding last act worthy of Wagner's *Götterdämmerung*—a twilight of the gods marking the collapse of a society or regime in chaos and disorder. Others suggested that Hitler's fleeing to the Alps would divert the Soviet troops and allow some two million Berliners to leave the city and escape having to fight the Soviets in the streets, but Goebbels disdained their suggestion. "If a single white flag is hoisted in Berlin," he declared, "I shall not hesitate to have the whole street and all its inhabitants blown up. This has the full authority of the Führer."

On April 20, leading members of the Nazi hierarchy gathered in the Berlin bunker for the last time, to mark Hitler's fifty-sixth birthday. Eva Braun served as the hostess. Her presence helped to lighten the depressing atmosphere in the bunker, but even she could not hold Hitler's violent outbursts in check. Despite his ashen face, trembling limbs, and stooped shoulders, he still inspired fear and respect.

The next day, Hitler ordered an all-out counterattack against the advancing Soviets—but the German army no longer existed. He finally admitted all was lost, but this was not his defeat. His inner circle, his army, the German people—everyone—had betrayed him. None of them was worthy of his leadership and sacrifices. He disclaimed all responsibility for the havoc he had brought upon them and the rest of humankind.

During the next few days, several members of Hitler's entourage left for the south, including Göring and Dr. Morell. By April 25, the Soviets had completely surrounded the city. That same day, Hitler received a telegram from Göring, who had established himself at the Berghof, Hitler's villa on the Obersalzberg, which he had built on the site of the Haus Wachenfeld with money earned from the royalties on *Mein Kampf.* Göring, in light of Hitler's decision to remain in Berlin, wrote,

"[D]o you agree that I, as your deputy . . . assume immediately the total leadership of the Reich with complete freedom of action at home and abroad." Göring wanted to negotiate for peace terms.

At first, Hitler shrugged his shoulders and said, "If the war is lost anyhow, it doesn't matter who does it." He soon changed his mind, however, and fired back a radio message to the Berghof, rescinding the earlier decree that had established Göring as deputy führer. "My freedom of action undisputed," he radioed. "I forbid any move by you in the direction indicated." Hitler soon worked himself into a frenzy over Göring's attempt to take over leadership of the Reich and ordered him arrested, stripped of all his offices, and expelled from the party.

Three days later, on April 28, Hitler received a telegram informing him that Heinrich Himmler had made an unsuccessful peace proposal to the Allies through the Swedish Consulate in Lübeck, a German port on the Baltic Sea. "Now Himmler has betrayed me!" Both Himmler and Göring would later take their own lives in prison by ingesting poison capsules.

Hitler blamed everyone but himself for the cataclysm. "Now nothing remains," he told two of his followers with tears in his eyes. "Nothing is spared to me. No loyalty, no honor is left; no disappointment, no treachery has been spared me. . . . Everything is over. Every possible wrong has been inflicted on me." That night, enemy shells struck the chancellery, tumbling its walls, and Soviet soldiers advanced to within a half-mile of the führerbunker. The time had come for him to prepare for death.

Earlier that afternoon, Hitler, in deference to Eva Braun's loyalty, announced his intention to marry her. Just before midnight, Eva, dressed in a long gown of black silk taffeta, and Hitler, wearing his uniform, exchanged wedding vows. After the ceremony, the new groom told eight guests—including Joseph Goebbels, his wife, Magda, and Martin Bormann—that his bride had asked to share his fate. In his last testament, dictated to his secretary, he said, "My wife and I choose to die in order to escape the shame of overthrow or capitulation. It is our wish that our bodies be burned immediately, here where I have performed the greater part of my daily work during the twelve years I served my people."

On April 29, Hitler began his final preparations. He appointed Goebbels to take his place as chancellor, but, to everyone's surprise, he named Grand Admiral Karl Dönitz of the Kriegsmarine to succeed him as head of the state and supreme commander. Early on the morning of April 30, 1945, he assembled his staff in the passageway and bid them a silent farewell with a handshake. For the next few hours, he conducted business in the usual way, while Eva remained in her room. At 2:30 PM, he ate lunch—a dish of spaghetti with a light sauce—with his two secretaries and his cook. After dining, he fetched his wife. With Eva, he said a second farewell to his staff, and the two of them returned to the führer's suite. His staff remained in the corridor outside, waiting silently.

Inside, Hitler and Eva sat on a couch together while she swallowed a capsule of potassium cyanide. Moments later, at about 3:30 PM, Hitler put the barrel of his Walther 7.65 millimeter pistol to his right temple and pulled the trigger. A picture of his mother at a very young age stood on a nearby console. His staff waited a few minutes, then entered the room, gathered up the two bodies, wrapped them in blankets, and carried them away.

Outside, amid exploding Soviet shells, Hitler's disciples laid the two corpses in a shallow depression of sandy soil in the chancellery garden and poured five

Hitler shakes hands with a member of his staff in the führerbunker shortly before killing himself. (National Archives)

cans of gasoline over them. A lighted rag ignited the fuel in a ball of flame. The attendants stood on the chancellery porch, partially sheltered from the shells, and came to attention to offer a final Nazi salute. A small column of black smoke rose from the burning corpses, which continued to burn for three hours. The charred remains were buried later in another part of the chancellery garden. The Nazi movement and the Third Reich—which Hitler boasted would last for a thousand years—died with him.

Days later, on May 7, 1945, Germany surrendered unconditionally to the Allies.

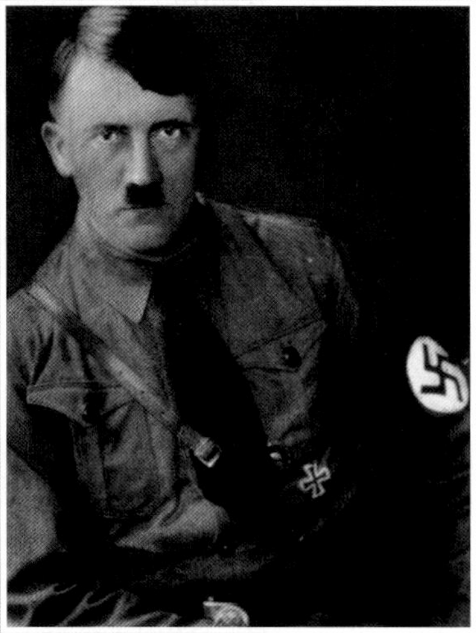

Timeline

1889	Adolf Hitler is born in Austria on April 20.
1903	Father dies.
1907	Mother dies.
1908-1913	Moves to Vienna; supports himself primarily by selling small paintings.
1914	World War I begins; Hitler enlists in the Bavarian army.
1916	Wounded in action on October 7.
1918	Wounded in action (gassed) and temporarily blinded on October 13; Germany signs an armistice on November 11.
1919	Treaty of Versailles signed on June 28, officially ending World War I.
1921	Becomes chairman of the Nazi Party.
1923	Munich Beer Hall Putsch; Hitler is arrested.
1924	Convicted of high treason and sentenced to five years in prison; writes the first volume of *Mein Kampf* (*My Struggle*) while in prison; pardoned and released in December.
1926	Second volume of *Mein Kampf* is published.
1932	Hitler becomes a German citizen.

1933	Hindenburg appoints Hitler chancellor of Germany on January 30.
1934	Hindenburg dies on August 2; Hitler combines offices of president and chancellor and names himself the führer of Germany.
1935	Hitler reintroduces a general military draft on March 16, in violation of the Treaty of Versailles; Hitler promulgates the Nuremberg Laws on September 15, severely limiting the rights of Jews.
1938	German troops invade Austria on March 12; Hitler takes the Sudetenland in September.
1939	On September 1, Germany invades Poland; Great Britain and France declare war on Germany on September 3.
1941	First Nazi death camp opens in Chelmno, Poland, in December; Japan bombs U.S. military installations at Pearl Harbor on December 7; Hitler declares war against the United States on December 11.
1942	Nazi leaders formulate plans for the Final Solution—the genocide of European Jews—at the Wannsee Conference on January 20; Nazis begin transporting Jews from Germany and other parts of western Europe to the death camp at Auschwitz in late March.
1944	Allies invade western Europe on June 6, D-Day.
1945	Hitler marries Eva Braun on April 28, then writes his last will and testament; Hitler and his wife commit suicide in his Berlin bunker on April 30; Germany surrenders unconditionally to the Allies on May 7; World War II ends in Europe.

⌁ SOURCES

CHAPTER ONE: Early Life

p. 10, "his most striking feature," Ian Kershaw, *Hitler, 1889–1936: Hubris* (New York: W. W. Norton, 1999), 12.

p. 10, "While he was not a . . ." Ibid.

p. 11, "It was especially my . . ." Ibid., 13.

p. 14, "Schoolwork was ridiculously . . ." Adolf Hitler, *Mein Kampf,* trans. by Ralph Manheim (Boston: Houghton Mifflin, 1971), 8.

p. 16, "I owe to Karl May . . ." Robert Payne, *The Life and Death of Adolf Hitler* (New York: Barnes & Noble Books, 1995), 27.

p. 16, "From then on I . . ." Hitler, *Mein Kampf,* 6.

p. 18, "I thought that once . . ." Ibid., 10.

p. 19, "The majority of them . . ." William L. Shirer, *The Rise and Fall of the Third Reich: A History of Nazi Germany* (New York: Simon & Schuster, 1960), 12.

p. 19, "gray-haired man . . ." Hitler, *Mein Kampf,* 14–15.

p. 19, "And indeed, though . . ." Ibid., 15.

p. 20, "He saw everywhere . . ." Shirer, *The Rise and Fall,* 15–16.

p. 20, 22, "I was so convinced . . ." Hitler, *Mein Kampf,* 20.

p. 22, "should some day become . . ." Ibid.

p. 22, "I have never seen . . ." Kershaw, *Hitler, 1889–1936*, 24.

p. 22, "was a dreadful blow . . ." Hitler, *Mein Kampf*, 18.

p. 22, "wanted to become . . ." Ibid.

CHAPTER TWO: The Aimless Years

p. 25, "To me Vienna . . ." Hitler, *Mein Kampf*, 21.

p. 25, "In this period my . . ." Ibid.

p. 26-27, "In this period there . . ." Ibid., 22.

p. 27, "On the very first day . . ." Alan Bullock, *Hitler: A Study in Tyranny,* Abridged ed. (New York: HarperCollins Publishers, 1991), 8.

p. 28, "Over and over again . . ." Ibid., 10.

p. 28, "When he got excited . . ." John Toland, *Adolf Hitler* (New York: Doubleday, 1992), 44.

p. 30, "The greater insight . . ." Hitler, *Mein Kampf*, 50.

p. 30, "spiritual and physical terror," Shirer, *The Rise and Fall*, 22.

p. 31, "profound thinker," Hitler, *Mein Kampf*, 98.

p. 32, "last great German . . ." Ibid., 69.

p. 32-33, "to make use of . . ." Ibid., 100.

p. 33, "If Dr. Karl Lueger . . ." Ibid., 121.

p. 34, "greatest transformation of all," Ibid., 55.

p. 34, "Once, as I was strolling. . ." Ibid., 56.

p. 34, "Wherever I went . . ." Ibid.

p. 35, "If the Jew wins . . ." Louis L. Snyder, *Encyclopedia of the Third Reich* (New York: Paragon House, 1989), 152.

p. 35, "Vienna was a hard . . ." Bullock, *Hitler*, 11.

p. 36, "too weak and unfit . . ." Snyder, *Encyclopedia of the Third Reich*, 152.

p. 36, "My joy and gratitude . . ." Hitler, *Mein Kampf*, 163.

CHAPTER THREE: Purpose in War

p. 37, "the greatest and most . . ." Hitler, *Mein Kampf*, 163.

p. 39, "At last there came . . . wounded Englishmen," Payne, *The Life and Death of Adolf Hitler,* 110–11.

p. 40, "The volunteers of . . ." Hitler, *Mein Kampf,* 165.

p. 41, "I was proposed . . ." Payne, *The Life and Death of Adolf Hitler,* 112.

p. 41, "As a dispatch runner . . ." Ibid., 113.

p. 42, "We all cursed him . . ." Konrad Heiden, *The Führer,* trans. by Ralph Mannheim (Edison, NJ: Castle Books, 2002), 74.

p. 44, "And so it had all . . ." Hitler, *Mein Kampf,* 204.

p. 48, "For me, the value . . ." Hitler, *Mein Kampf,* 208.

p. 48, "I started out with . . ." Ibid., 215–16.

CHAPTER FOUR: Victory in Defeat

p. 53-54, "Herr Harrer . . . was certainly . . ." Hitler, *Mein Kampf,* 356.

p. 54, "very significant . . ." Ibid.

p. 54, "feeble and uncertain . . ." Ibid.

p. 54, "Thus both men . . ." Ibid.

p. 54, "For this only beings . . ." Ibid.

p. 55, "There was often so . . ." Payne, *The Life and Death of Adolf Hitler,* 148.

p. 55, "a wolf had been born . . ." Ibid.

p. 56-57, "As National Socialists . . ." Hitler, *Mein Kampf,* 496–97.

p. 60, "So it will be with us . . ." Kershaw, *Hitler, 1889–1936,* 182–83.

p. 63, "The national revolution has begun . . ." Heiden, *The Führer,* 153.

p. 63, "Reichswehr and police are . . ." Ibid.

p. 63, "expression of a madman," Ibid.

p. 63, "Tomorrow will find . . ." Snyder, *Encyclopedia of the Third Reich,* 20.

p. 64, "The heavens will fall . . ." Toland, *Adolf Hitler*, 167.

p. 65, "Excellency, I must take you . . ." Otis C. Mitchell, "The Nazis' Failed 'Beer Hall *Putsch*,'" in *The Rise of Nazi Germany, Turning Points in World History*, ed. by Don Nardo (San Diego, CA: Greenhaven Press, 1999), 70.

p. 65, "You have your orders . . ." Ibid.

p. 65, "We never thought . . ." Ibid.

p. 66, "This is my attitude . . ." Heiden, *The Führer*, 165.

p. 66, "I believe that . . ." Bullock, *Hitler*, 63.

p. 67, "You may pronounce . . ." Heiden, *The Führer*, 167–168.

CHAPTER FIVE: Führer

p. 71, "The wild beast is checked . . ." Bullock, *Hitler*, 67.

p. 71, "Fight Marxism and Judaism . . ." Toland, *Adolf Hitler*, 209.

p. 72, "This is an absolutely . . ." Payne, *The Life and Death of Adolf Hitler*, 211.

p. 72, "Every man will have . . ." Snyder, *Encyclopedia of the Third Reich*, 106.

p. 72, "The wrangling must stop! . . ." Toland, *Adolf Hitler*, 208.

p. 73, "in him our people's will . . ." Heiden, *The Führer*, 219.

p. 77, "Neither Hitler nor I . . ." Toland, *Adolf Hitler*, 215.

p. 77, "was the foundation of . . ." Ibid., 216.

p. 79, "We are going into . . ." Kershaw, *Hitler, 1889–1936*, 303.

p. 82, "In the evening I would . . ." Bullock, *Hitler*, 76–77.

p. 85, "intelligent and quick to . . ." Toland, *Adolf Hitler*, 237.

p. 85, "my lovely siren . . ." Ibid.

p. 85-86, "In the summer of 1931 . . ." Robert Edwin Herzstein, and the Editors of Time-Life Books, *The Nazis, World War II.* (Alexandria, VA: Time-Life Books, 1980), 24.

p. 86, "alone, back bent, looking . . ." Joachim C. Fest, *Hitler,* trans. by Richard and Clara Winston (San Diego, CA: Harcourt Brace, 1974), 332.

p. 87, "Bohemian corporal," Kershaw, *Hitler, 1889–1936*, 371.

p. 87, "to transfer the . . ." Michael Burleigh, *The Third Reich: A New History* (New York: Hill and Wang, 2000), 143.

p. 87, "We are both old . . ." Ibid.

CHAPTER SIX: Seizure of Power

p. 90, "No power on earth . . ." Payne, *The Life and Death of Adolf Hitler*, 247.

p. 90, "with almost clairvoyant . . ." Fest, *Hitler*, 266.

p. 90, "By appointing Hitler . . ." Payne, *The Life and Death of Adolf Hitler*, 251–52.

p. 90-91, "of national resurrection . . ." Burleigh, *The Third Reich*, 153.

p. 91, "When Germany awoke . . ." Snyder, *Encyclopedia of the Third Reich*, 287.

p. 92, "We were prepared . . ." Richard J. Evans, *The Coming of the Third Reich* (New York: Penguin Press, 2004), 334.

p. 93, "a concentration camp . . ." Ibid., 344.

p. 98, "From my childhood . . ." Klaus P. Fischer, *Nazi Germany: A New History* (New York: Continuum, 1995), 285.

p. 100, "Forget the idea of a . . ." Snyder, *Encyclopedia of the Third Reich,* 31.

p. 101, "a strong impression," Fest, *Hitler*, 443.

p. 101, "impending revolt . . ." Ibid., 461.

p. 102, "present an outward . . ." Ibid., 462.

p. 103, "If Adolf wants . . ." Payne, *The Life and Death of Adolf Hitler*, 280.

p. 103-104, "The former Chief . . ." Kershaw, *Hitler, 1889–1936*, 516.

p. 104, "Let the nation know . . ." Fest, *Hitler*, 469.

p. 104, "In the next thousand . . ." Bullock, *Hitler*, 171.

CHAPTER SEVEN: *Lebensraum*

p. 106, "relations between . . ." Kershaw, *Hitler, 1889–1936*, 547.

p. 106, "Germany was . . . rearming . . ." Bullock, *Hitler*, 183.

p. 108, "repay the debt of . . ." Ibid., 188–89.

p. 109, "At this moment . . ." Toland, *Adolf Hitler*, 384.

p. 110, "to withdraw with . . ." Ibid., 388.

p. 111, "We are, and always . . ." Payne, *The Life and Death of Adolf Hitler*, 290.

p. 111, "The right of the . . ." Snyder, *Encyclopedia of the Third Reich*, 96.

p. 112, "[T]his Berlin-Rome line . . ." Toland, *Adolf Hitler*, 400.

p. 112, "Today, I must humbly . . ." Bullock, *Hitler*, 197.

p. 113, "He did not only . . ." Ian Kershaw, *Hitler, 1936–45: Nemesis* (New York: W. W. Norton, 2000), 29.

p. 114, "If the Führer was still . . ." Snyder, *Encyclopedia of the Third Reich*, 174.

p. 115, "son of the Austrian soil," Fest, *Hitler*, 546.

p. 115, "You, too, Your Excellency . . ." Ibid.

p. 116, "If other measures . . ." Ibid.

p. 116, "The Duce accepted . . ." Ibid., 547.

p. 116, "Then please tell Mussolini . . ." Ibid.

p. 116, "If Providence once . . ." Ibid., 548.

p. 117, "It is my unalterable . . ." Snyder, *Encyclopedia of the Third Reich*, 236.

p. 117-118, "The Germans in Czechoslovakia . . ." Toland, *Adolf Hitler*, 473.

p. 118, "We should be sorry . . ." Ibid.

p. 118, "We have come now . . ." Snyder, *Encyclopedia of the Third Reich*, 236.

p. 119, "I should still say . . ." Ibid.

p. 119, "I believe it is peace . . ." James Taylor and Warren Shaw, *The Penguin Dictionary of the Third Reich* (New York: Penguin Books, 1997), 55.

p. 120, "act side by side . . ." Norman Polmar and Thomas B. Allen, eds., *World War II: The Encyclopedia of the War Years 1941-1945* (New York: Random House, 1996), 614.

p. 120, "immediately . . . became involved . . ." Ibid.

CHAPTER EIGHT: Hitler's Wars

p. 122, "In the West it is essential . . ." Fest, *Hitler*, 599.

p. 123, "the numerous Polish attacks . . ." Payne, *The Life and Death of Adolf Hitler*, 364.

p. 123-124, "I am asking of no German . . ." Ibid.

p. 125, "My decision is unchangeable . . ." Shirer, *The Rise and Fall,* 618.

p. 126, "lives not worth living," Fischer, *Nazi Germany*, 633.

p. 127, "Poland shall be treated . . ." Snyder, *Encyclopedia of the Third Reich*, 97.

p. 127-128, "when the Allies were so . . ." Payne, *The Life and Death of Adolf Hitler*, 379.

p. 129, "so that, if the British Empire . . ." Bullock, *Hitler*, 341.

p. 130, "This is the greatest and . . ." Payne, *The Life and Death of Adolf Hitler*, 392.

p. 130, "Since England, despite her . . ." Shirer, *The Rise and Fall*, 753.

p. 132, "The German Wehrmacht . . ." Anthony Read, *The Devil's Disciples: Hitler's Inner Circle* (New York: W. W. Norton, 2004), 673.

p. 134, "Since I struggled through . . ." Bullock, *Hitler*, 380.

p. 137, "The war against Russia . . ." Snyder, *Encyclopedia of the Third Reich*, 199.

p. 137, "a final solution . . ." Ibid., 371.

CHAPTER NINE: Bringing Down the World

p. 138, "the responsibility for . . ." Toland, *Adolf Hitler*, 704.

p. 139, "fall through natural . . ." Snyder, *Encyclopedia of the Third Reich*, 372.

p. 139, "treated accordingly . . ." Ibid.

p. 139, "cozily around a fireplace," Toland, *Adolf Hitler*, 705.

p. 139, "After a while we . . ." Ibid.

p. 140, "Who was I to judge? . . ." Ibid.

p. 140, "refuse to go voluntarily . . ." Ibid.

p. 140, "We realize that this war . . ." Ibid.

p. 141, "He was a man . . ." Burleigh, *The Third Reich*, 497.

p. 142, "Surrender is forbidden. . . ." Editors of Time-Life Books, *WW II: The Time-Life History of World War II* (New York: Barnes & Noble, 1995), 207.

p. 143, "The front collapsed . . ." Erwin Rommel, *The Rommel Papers,* ed. by B. H. Liddell Hart, trans. by Paul Findlay (New York: Da Capo Press, 1953), 422.

p. 145, "intestinal exhaustion," Taylor and Shaw, *The Penguin Dictionary of the Third Reich*, 184.

p. 146, "What shall we do?" Editors of Time-Life Books, *WW II*, 301.

p. 146, "Make peace, you fools . . ." Ibid.

p. 147, "I am invulnerable . . ." David Welch, *The Hitler Conspiracies: Secrets and Lies behind the Rise and Fall of the Nazi Party* (Washington, DC: Brassey's, 2001), 171.

p. 148, "Panic will break out . . ." Toland, *Adolf Hitler*, 781.

p. 148, "The enemy has struck us . . ." Ibid., 782.

p. 149, "I have just made . . ." Editors of Time-Life Books, *WW II*, 316.

p. 149, "Here, out of the Ardennes . . ." Ibid.

p. 149, "If we reach the Meuse . . ." Sidney C. Moody Jr., and the Associated Press, *War in Europe* (Novato, CA: Presidio Press, 1993), 153.

p. 150, "We'll not capitulate. . . ." Kershaw, *Hitler, 1936–45*, 747.

CHAPTER TEN: Last Days

p. 151-152, "It was no longer . . ." Bullock, *Hitler*, 457-58.

p. 152, "However grave the . . ." Toland, *Adolf Hitler*, 846.

p. 153, "If the war is to be lost . . ." Payne, *The Life and Death of Adolf Hitler*, 541.

p. 153, "My Führer, I congratulate you! . . ." Fest, *Hitler*, 734.

p. 155, "If a single white flag . . ." Bullock, *Hitler*, 468.

p. 156, "[D]o you agree . . ." Payne, *The Life and Death of Adolf Hitler*, 544.

p. 156, "If the war is lost . . ." Ibid., 545.

p. 156, "My freedom of action . . ." Ibid.

p. 156, "Now Himmler . . ." Ibid., 546.

p. 156, "Now nothing . . ." Fest, *Hitler*, 740.

p. 157, "My wife and I . . ." Toland, *Adolf Hitler*, 883.

Bibliography

Barnett, Correlli, ed. *Hitler's Generals*. New York: Quill/William Morrow, 1989.

Bullock, Alan. *Hitler: A Study in Tyranny*. Abridged edition. New York: HarperCollins Publishers, 1991.

Burleigh, Michael. *The Third Reich: A New History*. New York: Hill and Wang, 2000.

Editors of Time-Life Books. *WW II: The Time-Life History of World War II*. New York: Barnes & Noble, 1995.

Evans, Richard J. *The Coming of the Third Reich*. New York: Penguin Press, 2004.

Fest, Joachim C. *Hitler*. Translated by Richard and Clara Winston. San Diego, CA: Harcourt Brace, 1974.

Fischer, Klaus P. *Nazi Germany: A New History*. New York: Continuum, 1995.

Heiden, Konrad. *The Führer*. Translated by Ralph Mannheim. Edison, NJ: Castle Books, 2002.

Herzstein, Robert Edwin, and the Editors of Time-Life Books. *The Nazis. World War II*. Alexandria, VA: Time-Life Books, 1980.

Heston, Leonard L., M.D., and Renate Heston, R.N. *The Medical Casebook of Adolf Hitler: His Illnesses, Doctors and Drugs*. Lanham, MD: University Press of America, 1980.

Hitler, Adolf. *Mein Kampf*. Translated by Ralph Manheim.

Boston: Houghton Mifflin, 1971.

Kershaw, Ian. *Hitler, 1936–45: Nemesis.* New York: W. W. Norton, 2000.

———. *Hitler, 1889–1936: Hubris.* New York: W. W. Norton, 1999.

Mitchell, Otis. "The Nazis Failed 'Beer Hall Putsch'" *The Rise of Nazi Germany. Turning Points in World History.* Edited by Don Nardo. San Diego, CA: Greenhaven Press, 1999.

Moody, Sidney C., Jr., and the Associated Press. *War in Europe.* Novato, CA: Presidio Press, 1993.

Payne, Robert. *The Life and Death of Adolf Hitler.* New York: Barnes & Noble Books, 1995.

Polmar, Norman, and Thomas B. Allen, eds. *World War II: The Encyclopedia of the War Years 1941-1945.* New York: Random House, 1996.

Read, Anthony. *The Devil's Disciples: Hitler's Inner Circle.* New York: W. W. Norton, 2004.

Rommel, Erwin. *The Rommel Papers.* Edited by B. H. Liddell Hart. Translated by Paul Findlay. New York: Da Capo Press, 1953.

Shirer, William L. *The Rise and Fall of the Third Reich: A History of Nazi Germany.* New York: Simon & Schuster, 1960.

Snyder, Louis L. *Encyclopedia of the Third Reich.* New York: Paragon House, 1989.

Speer, Albert. *Inside the Third Reich.* Translated by Richard and Clara Winston. New York: Galahad Books, 1995.

Taylor, James, and Warren Shaw. *The Penguin Dictionary of the Third Reich.* New York: Penguin Books, 1997.

Toland, John. *Adolf Hitler.* New York: Doubleday, 1992.

Welch, David. *The Hitler Conspiracies: Secrets and Lies behind the Rise and Fall of the Nazi Party.* Washington, DC: Brassey's, 2001.

❧ Web Sites

http://www.ushmm.org/
The United States Holocaust Memorial Museum maintains a large online exhibit and offers information about traveling exhibits and visiting the museum's permanent home in Washington, D.C.

http://www.auschwitz-muzeum.oswiecim.pl/html/eng/start/index.php
Auschwitz, one of the most infamous concentration camps, is now a museum and memorial. This Web site offers a virtual tour of the site along with information about the camp and those who lived—and died—there.

http://www.bbc.co.uk/history/war/wwtwo/
The British Broadcasting Company hosts an extensive site about World War II.

http://www.pbs.org/wgbh/nova/decoding/
During World War II, both sides used code to send messages. When the Allies broke the famous Enigma Code, it helped turn the tide of the war. This interactive Web site offers the story behind cracking the code and even the chance to create your own.

http://www.annefrank.org/
The online home of the Anne Frank House, with information about her famous diary and her family's attempt to hide from the Nazis.

✕ INDEX